LAY HOLD OF GOD'S POWER

GW00597769

Write if you must,
But – think on this –
Christ wrote but once
And then in dust.

John Oxenham

LAY HOLD OF GOD'S POWER

Moving the mountains in your life

Melvin Banks

Marshall Pickering
An Imprint of HarperCollinsPublishers

Marshall Pickering is an Imprint of
HarperCollins*Religious*
Part of HarperCollins*Publishers*
77–85 Fulham Palace Road, London W6 8JB

First published in Great Britain
in 1996 by Marshall Pickering

1   3   5   7   9   10   8   6   4   2

A catalogue record for this book is
available from the British Library

ISBN 0 551 03023 2

Printed and bound in Great Britain by
Caledonian International Book Manufacturing Ltd, Glasgow

CONTENTS

DEDICATION

I dedicate this book of power to my darling wife and partner in the ministry, Lilian, who for nearly 35 years of marriage has urged me to keep the Saviour and the message of the Blood of Christ and his Resurrection power foremost in my heart, life and ministry.

ACKNOWLEDGEMENTS

A special thank you to Mrs Gill Dyer, who did a fantastic job in typing, sorting, ordering and finalizing the manuscript, and to her husband Steve who so ably supported her.

THE PRESENCE OF CHRIST AND A MUSLIM KING

> I exhort first of all that ... giving of thanks be
> made for ... all who are in authority.
> 1 Timothy 2:1–2

The temperature was 120 degrees, and the streaming
vapour filled the air like a morning mist. I awoke to the
sound of the cockatoo, the annoying bites of many
mosquitoes during the long, hot night, and the knowledge that there was no bath or shower to welcome me.
But the cry of the far-off Mullahs, from 5 a.m., I had
now got used to.

The cry went on for an extra long time that morning,
as I hose-piped my sweaty body. (This was my daily
bath for eight weeks while on the mission to Malaysia.)
Then I remembered one of my Chinese pastor friends
telling me that it was Mohammed's birthday, a great
day in the Muslim calendar and in this predominantly
Islamic state. I soon discovered everything came to a
stop. Shops and theatres closed, taxis stood still – even
churches were not allowed to hold services.

Dr Paul Yonggi Cho, preaching to 20,000 in
Kuala Lumpur, had his crusade rally stopped for that
night by order of the government, with police and
troops enforcing the curfew. They had to turn
thousands away till the next day. But it was a miracle
that he or myself were allowed into the country at all to
preach to large crowds, as the World Pentecostal

Conference was banned from meeting in Kuala Lumpur.

I felt as if someone else stood by me that morning, and the words came to me: 'You will preach the Gospel in Rome also...' And again: 'You will preach the Gospel on Mohammed's birthday.' Am I going mad? Is this a trick of the mind? Are you overdoing it? Such were the very human thoughts which came to mind. But no, the presence, the glow, I could almost touch Him – Christ was at my side. It was glorious!

My nice, green Chinese tea arrived, and two pastors presented themselves on my doorstep. By now I had made some earnest phone calls including one to the Superintendent of Police. The worried look of the two men of God revealed their understandable fears that any pressure on the authorities would not only meet with stout resistance, but also create insurmountable problems for the church leaders there, in the jungles of South Malaya.

'Reverend Banky [my Chinese name],' they said, 'this is revival – we have reached with your faith and help thousands of idol-worshipping Chinese people. It's a miracle. But this is the law, no one has ever had a Gospel meeting on Mohammed's birthday. We must close down for the night and go on tomorrow.'

'This is a strict Islamic nation,' one went on. 'We have no power here. The Malay people control everything, we are second-class citizens here, we can be arrested if we are seen to be trouble-making.'

I turned to them. 'Let's make one more try,' I said. 'I promise if God grants it, it will be a miracle, a breakthrough, and things will be better for you than they were before. I will leave no problems behind for you – except,' I added with a smile, 'the problem of hundreds

of newborn babes in Christ to teethe, feed and teach.'
They both laughed.

'The phone, sir,' came the voice of my Chinese
servant. 'It's the local Chief of Police.' In broken
English, he made it clear that holding the meeting
was against the law and could not be allowed. The large
school building hired to us would be locked and
bolted! Some satisfaction seemed to come to the pastors
who were standing, looking and listening over my
shoulders.

'I will have to accept that,' I replied. 'But,' I warned,
'I am afraid I'm going to report this to the King.' The
Chief Officer suddenly gasped in shock. 'It is not
acceptable,' I went on. 'Here I am wanting to pray for
the King and the Royal Family to Almighty God and
you refuse me the opportunity. You are preventing
prayers on behalf of kings, strictly taught in the Bible
and the Koran!'

He came back forcibly, 'You are not Muslim and you
want to pray for our King?'

'Certainly I do, and you cannot prevent it,' I added.
'The Bible commands it.' Clearly embarrassed by this
turn in the debate, he hurriedly asked that I stay at
home till he could contact me.

The pastors were now almost beside themselves,
wondering if the security police were on their way
secretly to arrest us all, or if I was an angel in disguise
breaking the long-established Islamic mould. After
about an hour, which all of us (including my servant)
had spent prostrate on the floor before the Lord, the
phone rang again. Slowly, I lifted the receiver. It was the
Chief of Police for the whole district.

'I do very much say sorry, Reverend Banky,' he said. 'I
understand you very holy man, it will be OK for you to

hold meeting. This is very, very unusual, but we cannot prevent prayer for the King to the Almighty Allah. However, my police force must be present, to monitor prayers ... '

So that night, in jubilant spirit, I rose to the rostrum, my Chinese pastors behind me, still with much trepidation, as I led the prayers. There was standing room only in the huge public school hall. This was making history. All round the sides stood Chinese Police, including a local Inspector. I prayed a 20 minute prayer, for the King Mujab Haidi, El Kelah, Mab Aliegh, and Princess so-and-so, and Queen so-and-so, until I had covered the whole family. At the end the police nodded their heads. The Superintendent, by now in attendance, signalled and they all left. We sang in Chinese, in Malay, then in Indian. I preached the Gospel and 100 were soundly converted, and healings continued till midnight. When we finished, the Chinese pastors were all exhausted and laughing.

'They cannot arrest us now,' I said, 'for Mohammed's birthday is over – it's five past midnight!'

It is amazing what one or two small believers or unknown preachers can do with the presence of Christ and in obedience to Him. I heard later that from that day things were much easier for the churches and pastors in that huge jungle area. They have never looked back! You see the presence of Christ can change everything. A few men and women of faith can change a nation; one person with the presence of Jesus can achieve more than vast conferences of believers.

LET GOD OPEN THE GATE

'Now faith is the substance of things hoped for, the evidence of things not seen' (Hebrews 11:1). Faith is a

4

gift from God, gladly given and kept alive by the Spirit.

The songwriter Oscar Eliason wrote: 'Got any rivers you think are uncrossable? Got any mountains you can't tunnel through?' He answered these questions by saying, 'God specializes in things thought impossible.' That's good news, because every Christian faces obstacles along life's pathway, and walking in God's will doesn't guarantee that the way will be easy. That's why we must trust God and go forward in faith.

At the entrance to a local hospital parking lot there is an automatic gate. It is designed to raise when a car activates a hidden sensor near the entrance. When I drive up the ramp leading to that gate, it remains down, firmly blocking the entrance. But as I get close to it, the arm swings up and I proceed right through. If I were to park my car a few yards away from the entrance, it would stay closed. Only as I move forward does it open.

Is there some barrier across your path just now?

Someone has said, 'If God built a bridge a yard ahead, it could not be a bridge of faith.' It's that first step into the unseen that proves we have faith. Abraham, for example, 'went out, not knowing where he was going' (Hebrews 11:8). He was obeying God and relying on Him. Abraham's task was to go; God's was to clear the path. If you have been walking in obedience to the Lord, yet you have been stopped by a closed gate, take the step today!

Faith is the gate between man's peril and God's power.

You cannot see today the hidden meaning
Of My command, but you the light shall gain;
Walk on in faith, upon My promise leaning,
And as you're going all shall be made plain.

A tremendous moving of the Spirit on an individual can move mountains of troubles, obstacles and hindrances. Jesus' presence never leaves the people the same as they were before. Even as you read these words you can feel a stirring, cutting, deeply disturbing shaking of God's mighty Spirit. His presence lifts us up beyond the human realm, above ourselves.

The presence of Jesus is like the story from Bunyan's *Pilgrim's Progress*, when Christian enters the castle and sees some men trying to put out a fire which keeps bursting into flame again. The reason behind the fire in the other room was that someone was using bellows to stir the fire up, so it was kept at top intensity!

The man leaning over the fire with His bellows was our Lord Jesus. His presence stirs us to have the faith of God, to do the impossible. When Jesus saw Jairus's daughter lying dead, he said, 'She is not dead, but sleepeth,' and He went on to raise her from the dead. Why did He say, 'she ... sleepeth'? Because He did not see her as dead! That is faith. He saw beyond the human eye. Have God's faith. Astounding, life-giving faith brings down the glorious presence. God will come down for a man of faith, a few believing people, the Spirit comes down and rejuvenates us.

God honours faith – faith honours God. God comes and moves with the men who move. T. L. Osborne used to say: 'Faith moves the hand of God, and the hand of God moves everything else!' Impossibilities become possible, this leads us to victory, faith is the new order that God sees and acts upon. Unbelief means we are powerless, no presence, no glory. Faith is contagious. Faith brings in the Mighty God.

Faith is accepting the call to 'come and see' (John 1:39). To invite Jesus in is to invite heaven into your life and home. His appearance pre-empts any lack I have, His care is beyond price. I've asked God in prayer, 'that my life be an ever-open door to you Lord'. As one ninety-year-old Pentecostal preacher puts it: 'His presence is finding, following and feasting … !' Life is enhanced, surprizing and mostly very exciting when Jesus plays a part in it.

The ABC of faith is simple, in that it is confidence in Christ as a person, resting on what He is, not on what He does. We believe and are sure without seeing, that faith in our Lord makes all miracles possible, the greatest being that He is ever and always present – if we are willing!

Of course the value of faith is determined by the object of your faith; not faith itself, but rather what or whom faith is reliant on. At Tarn Howes, in Cumbria's Lake District, on a winter's day, after freezing weather, the lake is frozen solid. It may take some faith to step out on the lake, you first put your toes on it and gently press around the edge a little. You make sure it is worthy of your trust – strong enough to take your weight! But as soon you are skating, it is not your faith holding you up but the strength or reliability of what is beneath your feet – the ice does it for you. Go along in the summer and try to walk on the lake, it doesn't matter how much faith you have, the water will not keep you up. So our reliance is not on faith itself, but on the Lord God who is faithful to keep His word. He is reliable, unchanging, able to 'do above all that we ask or think'.

Faith reveals what sort of people we are. By our works they see our faith. By our acts, exploits and godly achievements faith is revealed.

When Ulysses came home after 20 years of wandering adventure, his wife said, 'It isn't Ulysses.' So he took a bow, so tough that no man could use it, and bent it until the string touched his ear. Then they knew who he was. Jesus said, 'the works that I do in My Father's name bear witness of Me,' and He added, 'the works that I do you shall do also ... Greater works than these shall you do.' By faith we can do greater works through the Holy Spirit working in us. What a challenge! What a power we have in our hands and our lives!

FAITH WILL MOVE THE WORLD

After President James Garfield was shot in 1881 it was decided to take him to the seaside in New Jersey in the hope that his fight for life would be successful. He was to be transported by railway but the line ended short of the destination. It was decided to extend the line, but the owner of a lovely house and farm refused to let them build it through his land. When someone said, 'But it's for the President,' the man replied, 'If it's for the President, you can run your railway right through the middle of my house.'

Smith Wigglesworth used to say: 'For a man of faith God will do anything.' Faith will move the world. 'Without faith it is impossible to please God', for 'God is a rewarder of those that diligently seek him' (Hebrews 11:6). God will break a million chains to set you free, and others free through you, for a little faith.

Faith changes the whole atmosphere – when believing people utilize this great gift, it brings the instant reality of a Christ's presence with us. Sometimes we cannot move, we are stuck on our knees or seats – He is so real. I can even see Him, touch Him!

Of course it's not the intensity of the meetings that causes this. The press often describe how a 'highly charged emotion, a moving, deeply touching feeling pervaded the building'. But really it's the intensity of personal love and devotion. It's not flashing sentiment, or passing emotion, or grand sensationalism, for there is no horizon to the vision of faith. Nothing is impossible when we have the divine presence. The glory of God comes into immediate view.

OVERCOME

Faith is focused supremely on Jesus. We live in a storm-tossed age, the night of terror is about to begin, the storm will soon engulf the whole world. The Lord of the world to come can be present with us as the days darken. In a world buckling and bulging, God wants to teach you the lesson of trusting in all circumstances. Don't let the acids of bitterness, jealousy, feelings of inadequacy, depression or rejection eat away at you inside. Seven times the Risen Lord said to the seven churches in Revelation one word – 'OVERCOME'. This is the way to face the trials and demands and win through, grasping the promise of His presence, laying hold of His power.

Paul writes in 1 Corinthians 3:16 (NIV): 'Don't you know that you yourselves are God's temple, and that God's Spirit lives in you … ?' And in Revelation 21:3 (NIV) we have the promise of His presence day and night: 'Now the dwelling of God is with men, and He will live with them. They will be His people, and God

Himself will be with them and be their God.' With this presence we become specialists about Jesus, people who magnify Jesus, who reveal His works.

Everything you need you can find in Him. If you're hungry, He is the Bread of Life. If you're thirsty, He is your Water of Life. If you are empty, He is your Eternal Life.

In Malaysia with the King, Christ's presence met every circumstance and problem – achieving the hitherto impossible! Whatever mountains are in your way, with Christ's presence you can move them.

2

I Meet Christ on a River Bank

It was some time after my return to the United Kingdom from Malaysia that I stood on the river bank at Uphill, Somerset, on a cold winter's afternoon. The breeze bit into my face as I scanned the mouth and the low tide, as the water (well down for the wintertime) trickled into the sea. It was nearly 54 years after my miracle on that spot, and I had been back only once, some 20 years previously. But it meant so much more to me that day.

I had promised to bring my mother here, but whenever in nearby Weston-super-Mare, where I often drove her for a day out by the sea, she had always put it off. For some reason she did not want to take me back there. I often wondered what lay behind this reluctance.

She had gone to heaven five weeks earlier. I had returned from a month of busy church planting crusades in Belgium, to discover she had died 30 hours before. Now I felt her love closer than ever. For at this spot, on the river bank – then, in 1940, the trickle was a raging torrent – my father fished about in the waters trying to find me. With horror and tears, rapidly thrashing about, twisting, turning, groping under the water, to the right and left, he probed for my childish form.

Finally, grabbing my waist, he pulled me out, up the slippery bank – sliding, losing a foothold, exhausted. He picked his way on to firmer, more level ground, shaking me, opening my mouth, bending me, working hard to flush out the water. After some minutes he looked grim. Although it was a summer's day, I was ice cold, with no breath, no pulse. His horrific stare told it all, those nearby commented. He shook his head in silence. Mother sobbed, fell on her knees, held my cold, lifeless body in her arms. 'O God,' she cried quietly, 'he is yours. Give me back my child ... you can have him ... I will give him to you ... but let me have him back ... '

I must have been 10 minutes in her gentle arms, but, as suddenly as the whole fateful episode had begun, it ended. An amazed father broke the silence:

'Hey! He's warm, there's colour in his cheeks, I can feel, yes, I can feel his heartbeat,' he shouted, like a man who had suddenly discovered a gold-mine. Then, holding on to my tiny wrist he declared, 'The pulse is going fast – it's wonderful!'

At first, Mother could not speak, but only weep quietly, and hold me firmly to her breast. 'It's a miracle,' she said, thoughtfully and passively. 'We must get him to hospital,' Dad rejoined.

Soon I was in the Weston General Hospital Children's Ward undergoing all sorts of checks, but there was nothing for them to do, for GOD HAD DONE IT. I was out running about the next day, fit and well!

The sound of the seagulls brought me again to consciousness, and my thoughts returned to the 1990s. George Hamnett, a good friend of mine who was accompanying me on this visit, said, 'I can imagine it all, Melvin – the first of a thousand miracles in your life.' That was certainly true, for my mother had the presence of Christ with her that day. The God of Heaven chose to be there, and touch her lips, see her loving heart, hear her prayer, and make it the first of many miracles that would startle millions the world over.

Where are the people with the presence of Christ in them to pray prayers like that today? Denominational leaders seem obsessed with changing church structures. Every major church grouping in the UK has been going through some form of organisational remodelling in the past five years. It has brought none of them revival, and in some cases made things worse for their members. Even the stronger fundamentalist bodies, like the Pentecostals, seem to have spent much of their time reforming the system with little result.

Still millions go to hell. Still the kingdom of darkness waits to be broken down. Still the commission of Christ waits to be fulfilled in evangelizing all men.

It is not only making more people Christians but rather *making Christians more Christian*. That's what we need to be working on. It is imperative that we carry with us the presence of Christ.

PRESENCE LOST

Martin Luther said: 'There are only two men in history, Adam and Christ, all other men hang from their girdles.' In the Garden of Eden the special communion, fellowship and relationship God had with man was broken, the curse came on the human race. As the Chinese Philosopher put it: 'There are only two good men left in the world: one is dead and the other is not yet born!' Sin fell on man, and everything has gone wrong since. James the Apostle said: 'Death came by sin.' Paul declared: 'Death reigned from Adam' (Romans 5:14), and again, 'the wages of sin is death' (Romans 6:23).

Someone once wrote a play called *Death Takes a Holiday*, but the fact is that it never does. Death is always active and has been ever since Adam's fall. Anne Boleyn, second Queen to Henry VIII of England, said as she faced the scaffold, 'Death doth draw me, there is no remedy.' The presence of God lost – death, sin, hell and darkness has replaced it. As Wordsworth put it, 'Dark and more dark the shades of evening fell'.

I was once invited to speak to 1,500 teenagers dancing into the night at the Newcastle Essoldo Dance Hall on Tyneside. They gave me five minutes to bring them a Christian message and a Gospel song. After a rousing praise and Gospel item, I spoke. At first some teenagers giggled, shouted, coughed loudly (some of the alcohol protesting no doubt?), but soon silence fell on this huge crowd of youth, as I warned of sin, the affect of the decadence of their hearts, the dangers of drugs, immorality, AIDS, and a wasted life away from their Maker. It was short and sharp, but effective. I can see now the hundreds of upturned faces in the semi-darkness. Empty hearts and minds, forsaken, mostly loveless, yearning for something deeper. Many tried to talk to us as we made our way to the Manager's office for coffee afterwards and a word of thanks from him and his staff. Many questions were asked of our team and helpers – the quest and hunger were titanic. We were taking the presence of God to within a yard of hell.

Man was made to live in the presence of God. Sin,

deviousness and disobedience drove our first parents out of the Garden. They did not walk out, they were *driven* out. Genesis 3:24 tells us: 'So He drove out the man; and He placed Cherubims at the east of the Garden of Eden, and a flaming sword which turned every way, to guard the way to the tree of life.'

Bishop Lightfoot said, 'Our first parents made the great mistake that modern man makes everyday.' Hugel, the German thinker, put it: 'History has taught man nothing, except that he has learnt nothing.' We make the same mad decisions in every age, the same failure.

Man has lost touch with God ever since. Now in the deepest of deep darkness, with the peak of the storm about to come upon us, man is as far away as ever from knowing His God, and in this dethronement of God, the Church has lowered its sights, standards and desires. If ever believers should be living in the anointing, living in the presence of God, it is today. The world is torn apart – bottomless recession, broken lives, ruined careers, bankruptcies, shattered marriages, emotional abuse and countless personal tragedies. We face the sombre, joyless, unromantic reality of a nation and society in deep trouble. John said: 'The world is passing away and the lusts of it.'

OKAY GOD – NOW WHAT?

During a terrible hurricane in the USA recently, thousands of homes were flattened. A big sign was put up in the midst of the rubble: 'OKAY GOD – NOW WHAT?'

In a time of so much security there is much insecurity. In a time of plenty so many people with nothing.

Sadness, broken hearts and despair, not only among the thousands of homeless, but amongst the affluent and well-off too. Many have lost their way in our society, in a vicious circle of 'keeping up with the Joneses'. Materialism is a bad god, making people turn on one another, breeding selfishness, greed and covetousness.

It's rather like the old lady who had not been on the London Underground for many years. Unused to the bustle and fast pace, she found herself on the Circle Line, which goes round and eventually comes back to the same place again. Each time she very nervously came to get off the train, the crowd would push out and the doors would close before she could pluck up courage to step off. Hence three hours later she had been round three times and not got off. The humorous cockney story goes she is still going round three years later!

FAILED

A TV show recently reported that 95 per cent of people would not give to the street beggars in the UK. Multitudes are going round and round in a circle – careless of the needs of others, passing the wounded man by, unlike the Good Samaritan who risked all to save him. Hedonism is rampant, society is eaten up with itself. The system seems to have no answer to the dilemma. Social workers, psychologists, vicars, counsellors, the medical world – all have failed.

Job said, 'they have chosen their own way' (Job 29:25). David said, 'their way is their folly' (Psalm 49:13). Jeremiah said, 'the ways of the people do mourn' (Lamentations 1:4). Moses records in

Numbers 11:10: 'the people wept throughout their families'.

The Church has settled for not only less than the best, but the bottom of the scale of its inheritance. We have the answer but have failed society, and left people without hope. Jeremiah said: 'Why do you sit still? assemble yourselves, rise up ... ' (Jeremiah 8:14). And again, 'Why do you keep the good news to yourselves?' (2 Kings 7:9)

God has promised His people His personal presence. A Church or people of God with that presence and anointing is the only answer for starving, broken and crying humanity.

A little boy, writing to some missionaries, was told by his Sunday School teacher: 'Do not expect an answer as they are very busy people, but write telling them you are praying for them.' The little boy wrote and sent his letter to the missionaries, which read:

Dear Rev. Smith
   I am just writing to let you know I am thinking of you every day, and also praying for you a lot, but be sure I am not expecting an answer.
                                        Your pal Jim

The Church is not living in the radiant expectation of an answer, not living in the glorious presence of the King of Kings.

PERSON TO PERSON

Salvation is a person to person call. When I was crusading on huge missions in rural Malaysia, I had been in the jungle for almost two months, during which time I had not had a bath or a shower. Lizards ran over my bed, I was bitten by mosquitoes fifteen times in one night. Praying for the sick till two o'clock in the morning, being woken up at five o'clock by the Mullahs chanting prayers from the minarets in the distance. One day after a tasty Chinese meal, I asked what the meat was I had just eaten, and they told me it was 'young rat'!

I had not seen my wife in all that time, so I tried to phone her across those 5,000 miles. In the jungle it was the old, crackly colonial-type heavy black phones at that time. Finally, after putting in for a call six hours previously, I got through to her on a person to person call. How marvellous to hear her voice, although so quiet and remote after such a long period.

Jesus is a personal God reaching into the person of man. Salvation began in the heart of God and is not complete till it is received in your heart. 'He is the light that lighteth every man that cometh into the world' (John 1:9).

After that amazing event, at Uphill, Somerset, when I first met the presence of God, my mother, of course, brought me up faithfully to follow Him. From that day on, going to Church of England Sunday School, showing me how to pray, loving me, guiding me, even through my early rebellious teens to my conversion in a Billy Graham crusade in 1955. On through the years of preaching round the Wiltshire villages, into Bible College in London, into my days as Assistant Pastor, then as a fully ordained Minister, then into the signs and wonders Word Ministry, into faith, miracles, healing and revival. She passed into the presence of the Lord gloriously in her seventy-ninth year, dying without pain or disease, passing within hours, with no suffering. A light went out in the West of England the day she passed over that thousands miss today.

Although I've had the privilege of carrying the Good News of Christ to 34 nations of the world and to millions of people, occasionally something funny happens, like in the church where I was due to preach for three nights. I had never been in that area of England before, and the church leaders had not met me. The local Christians had put out 20,000 personal invitations for the meetings. I arrived 20 minutes early for the service and stood just inside the church door as hundreds poured in to get a seat. Three men in black suits (I guessed they were the local elders) anxiously looked at their watches and muttered to one another, peeping over the crowd and out of the doors. Suddenly one spied me, and approaching shook my hand. 'Are you the Evangelist … ?' He had not recognized me, although he had seen a picture of me 20,000 times, plus on TV, in the papers, and on 200 posters!

It's nice sometimes not to be recognized! But worse than this – many don't recognize the moving of God in their lives. They do not see the touches of God on their lives, they let the blessings slip, they let the light fade.

Jesus is always the same! His mercy, grace, power, gifts and inheritances for us are always on offer. His miraculous healing ministry has not dimmed with the ages, or grown weak through the centuries, His presence is awaiting us. DON'T MISS HIS PRESENCE. He is knocking on your heart's door.

Holman Hunt's famous painting of Jesus, 'The Light of the World', shows the popular image of the Saviour coming out of the darkness of the vineyard, to the door with no outside handle, overgrown with weeds and neglected, the heart closed to God in apathy. Only recently did I notice the foot in the painting. It is pointing slightly away and by it lies a fallen apple, lost fruit, lost opportunities, lost sweetness, lost by the dormant, idle, indifferent heart. Christ, not willing to knock forever, is already on the move, on down the road, on to another soul and another town, another age, another generation ... Now is the time to be in His presence, to welcome Him in, to take His hand, to bear His fruit, to know His blessings. He wants to restore His lost presence to His Church.

I've said many a time, crying before God, prior to going on stage to preach His Word before a desperate, needy congregation – hundreds of sick, dying people waiting for a miracle and a sceptical press waiting to see what blood they could spill – I've called on God: 'If You desert me today all is lost, Lord, let me feel Your presence.' I've said with the people of Moses' day, 'If Your presence does not go with us, do not send us up from here!' (Exodus 33:15)

This is the distinguishing mark of the truly anointed believer, as we see in Exodus 33:16: 'What else will distinguish me and Your people from all the other people on the face of the earth?' In it lies true reality, and this lost world then sees we have been with the Master, His mighty anointing is on us and they cry out: 'God is with you in everything you do … !' (Genesis 21:22)

We are His chosen – we have His presence. We are not of the world. We left Egypt behind. 'I am the Lord your God, who brought you out of Egypt so that you would no longer be slaves to the Egyptians; I broke the bars of your yoke and enabled you to walk with heads held high' (Leviticus 26:13).

May we live like the King's Children. May we dwell constantly in His presence. May you be set free from religious traditionalism, become triumphant, walk with the sovereign God, and with Jesus find that everything is a piece of cake. It began for me on that river bank, long ago. I want to share with you how delightful it is today, and what I've learned, to help you reign with the King, to win all the time, lose every burden. Grasp these truths of God and your life will be astounding

3

THE INCOMPARABLE CHRIST

Sometimes I go out with a pastor in a town where I am holding a mission, to pray for some poor bedfast sick person. I walk into the house, and often the whole atmosphere is full of caution or doubt. I've got to start at the very beginning, it's back to basics.

It's like a great revival meeting with one person. They have completely lost hope, they are full of negativism. It's blood, sweat and tears imparting faith from the Word into them for 10 to 15 heart-breaking minutes. Then after a mighty back-breaking prayer of faith, I know the work is done, the sick recipient is singing with new life, full of hope and joy, even in their body the pain is vanishing, often although bedfast for months they get up and walk around the room, weak, but with ever flowing new strength coming into their body from the Saviour and Healer, Jesus Christ.

YOU'VE LOST IT!

I am there only a short time, I believe in the scripture: 'thy light shall break forth as the morning, and thy health shall spring forth speedily' (Isaiah 58:8). I see an instant salvation and a miracle. But then the pastor, after I have left, goes on with such long prayers and scriptures, he moans and twists and turns over the person, so that they are back to where they were when we first walked into the house. He goes and undoes everything with his 'comforting admonishings'. 'Oh Lord, don't let our dear sister get discouraged if this symptom comes,' or, 'Let her see the will of the Lord, help her in her pains ... etc., etc.' She finishes up as discouraged as she was formerly. Oh God, help us with such attitudes and prayers and such low faith. Not every minister is like that – some have more faith than I have, thank God!

But I like Martin Luther's famous prayer: 'O Lord, deliver me from my enemies and also, O God, deliver me from my friends.' I go down the street with such a pastor saying, 'You've lost it for her; you've lost it for us ... !' God is looking for those who will stand immovable in trust. As the Lord said to Ezekiel, 'I sought for a man among them that should make up the hedge, and stand in the gap before Me for the land ... but I found none' (Ezekiel 22:30). Isaiah complained that the people had lost it: 'And there is none that calleth upon Thy Name, that stirreth up himself to take hold of Thee' (Isaiah 64:7).

We must have positive, beseeching, earnest prayers to get the victory. A man was carried in on a bed to a meeting in Brighton on the South Coast of England, all crippled and paralysed in various limbs. After he was suddenly, miraculously healed, the question asked by the media so often came to the fore:

'How is this done?'

'It's God answering prayer,' I replied.

'But by what power?'

'BY THE WOUNDS, BRUISES AND SUFFERING OF CHRIST ON THE CROSS!' I returned, emphatically.

Grasp this truth and you will not lose the blessing.

23

We must utterly have faith in the fact that the Son of God is the one who exercises God's sovereign rule over the universe – and in all His subjects.

THE WHOLE TRUTH

The Letter to the Hebrews is a wonderful place to begin an exploration of the incomparable nature of Christ and His unique role in the universe. Hebrews 1:3 tells us: 'The Son is the radiance of God's glory and the exact representation of His being.' The first claim made here is that God has spoken and has revealed Himself to us. If God had remained silent, enshrouded in impenetrable mystery, our plight would be hopeless. We would be left to grasp after the truth about God as best we could. The Greeks realized the problem which this creates.

We humans are finite and imperfect, but God is infinite and perfect. So how can we expect to come to know the truth about Him and comprehend it with our unaided reason? One school of Greek theology concluded that the best we can do is say what God is *not* by contrast with finite, imperfect humanity.

In contrast, the Jews claimed that God had revealed Himself to humankind through the succession of Hebrew prophets from Moses onwards. The writer does not dismiss this claim. He accepts it and builds on it.

The prophets did indeed convey a true revelation from God but it came 'at many times and in various ways' (Hebrews 1:1). It was a fragmentary and unsystematic revelation. Each prophet had a true message from God, but it was only part of the truth, the part that was needed in their time and situation.

No prophet proclaimed the full, rounded truth of God.

With Jesus it was different. He did not bring part of the truth – he was the Truth in its fullness. In Him, God did not display some *facet* of Himself, but displayed *Himself* in as full a way as we can comprehend. This is why Jesus is more than a prophet, He is the Son. The prophets grasped something of the mind of God and so proclaimed the Word of God. Jesus is the mind of God – the Word become flesh.

The writer is not belittling the prophets, but stressing the supremacy of Jesus. He is not saying that there is any break between the revelation in the prophets and that in Jesus. He is asserting a continuity but one that ends in consummation.

Jesus sums up, brings together, and completes that revelation. It achieves fullness of expression in Him. It is properly integrated in Him. He is the final and definitive revelation. That is why Jesus' coming marks the arrival of 'the last days' (Hebrews 1:2).

THE LAST DAYS

I am sure the great miracles we are seeing, the rapid evangelization of so many people in the UK at this time is a sure sign of the latter times. Just as Christ's immediate personal presence in the Gospels witnessed such gifts of personal, sudden, instant salvation and healing, so His personal presence now and near coming back to the earth visibly, begets many marvellous similar wonders.

For Zacchaeus, Jesus stood under the tree and called and, 'he made haste and came down and received Him joyfully'. For the Ethiopian leader in

25

the Gaza desert with Philip the evangelist it was in seconds that he gripped hold of His Maker, 'I believe Jesus Christ is the Son of God,' within seconds he had made his affirmation and the evangelist soon found a place to baptize him, even in a desert.

For the Philippian jailer it was instant, he cried out under God's conviction, 'What must I do?' Paul and Silas soon told him the Good News, and 'That very hour he believed and was baptized, he and all his household.' Not bad in an hour to win, convert, confirm, assure and baptize a whole family!

In Basle, Switzerland, recently, as I was holding crowded meetings in a large public hall, scores were finding Christ as Saviour, a Roman Catholic lady was amongst them. Her daughter had been trying to win her for some years, but she did not grasp anything. But in seconds, as I gave the appeal to repent and come to Christ, I said simply, 'The Roman Catholic can come, the Jewish can come, the Protestant, the Muslim can come ... ' It flashed like lightning in her spirit and she ran to the Cross, and was instantly born again and soaks herself in God's Word every day.

This harvest is a sign of the last days.

In Hebrew thought, 'the last days' meant the coming of the age of fulfilment in which all the promises in the prophets would come to fulfilment. This fulfilment is found in Jesus.

As well as claiming that God has revealed Himself in Christ, the writer to the Hebrews also asserts that Jesus was the agent in creation: 'In these last days he has spoken to us by his Son, whom he appointed heir of all things, and through whom he made the universe' (Hebrews 1:2). The early Christians came to see the Son in this role because of the identification of Jesus with the Word and Wisdom of God, both of which played a part in creation (Genesis 1; Psalm 33:6; Proverbs 8:22ff.; John 1:3 and Colossians 1:16).

The word used here for 'the universe' is 'the ages'. I think the significance of this is that the Son is seen as Creator not just of the universe as a physical structure, but also as an entity that goes through successive phases, that has a history. If you like, the Son is creator of history, of time, as well as of matter and space.

Jesus is also one with God. In much Greek thought, there was a strong separation between matter and spirit. This led to the idea that the creator of matter had to be an inferior spiritual being, perhaps even an evil one. The writer of Hebrews dispels any such idea by declaring that the Son, the Creator, is truly God. He does this by identifying Him with God's glory and with God's nature.

THE WORD BECAME FLESH

Before anything else existed there was Christ with God. He has always been alive and is Himself God. He created everything ... eternal life is in Him ... His life is the light to all mankind ... that shines through the darkness, and the darkness can never extinguish it ... the One who is the true light arrived ... but although He made the world, the world did not recognize Him ... only a few would welcome Him ... but to all who received Him, He gave the right to become children of God ... Christ took our human nature and lived here on earth

27

among us and was full of loving forgiveness and truth, the glory of the only Son of the Heavenly Father. (John 1:1–14, Living Bible)

St Paul writes that 'God was in Christ reconciling the Father unto Himself' (2 Corinthians 5:19). Origen, the Church Father, called Him the 'eternal generation'. George Sweeting wrote: 'He had no beginning, He *was* the beginning.' Spurgeon, described Him as 'the infinite infant'.

George Duncan wrote 'the incarnation is the miracle that lies at the heart of Christianity'. The King of Kings has visited this world of ours. 'He made Himself of no reputation,' wrote St Paul, ' ... took upon Him the form of a servant, and was made in the likeness of men.' He did indeed come down to earth. John Wesley proclaimed that 'Christ never divested Himself of His essential Deity'. He was in the shape of man walking these roads of this world but truly God. He put a self-imposed limitation upon His divinity for a while, He restricted Himself to a human body. The theologians called it the 'hypostatic union', or the two natures blending in one truly God and truly man. I call it the emptying of Himself of the exercise of the prerogative of Deity. The glorious God came to earth, Colossians called Him the 'first-born of every creature' (Colossians 1:15). He was God with the Father before creation.

Huber, the Swiss naturalist, illustrated it, when playing with ants on the ground in the garden one day. His mum noted, 'The ants are running all over because they think you are going to hurt them.'

'They are frightened of me?' Huber exclaimed

'Yes, but you wouldn't hurt them ... '

'Certainly not,' he replied, 'but how can I let them know that I am so fond of them, except by becoming an ant?'

So our Creator became our Saviour. He came into this world. Martin Luther wrote: 'Rejoice in the Incarnation, trust that it occurred for through it we are no longer aliens under God's wrath.' God spoke upon this earth and still speaks to our world. He became a servant that He might redeem us. As Bishop John Pearson put it, 'Christ was in the form of God, before He was in the form of man.'

THIS IS THE KING SPEAKING

As a small boy I remember in the dark, early 1940s, my father away in the War, my mum let me stay up very late. The King of England was speaking to the nation at that sad, crucial time. I was very sleepy but I struggled to stay awake, Why? Because the King was going to speak to me. Finally on the crackly old wireless, I heard the King, encouraging us. I can barely remember his words, but they went something like this: 'THIS IS THE KING SPEAKING TO YOU ... these are dark and trying days, our loved ones are far away, but we must not give up hope ... One day if we pull together we will have victory. Europe will again be free, evil will be defeated, and our sons and fathers will come home again. Don't forget to say your prayers ... '

It was unforgettable, the King had talked in my ear. So God speaks to us today, He came to us, He dwells in us. In Revelation, John writes that 'the tabernacle of God has dwelt amongst men'. The Holy God is with us, and now *in* us.

The writer to the Hebrews also claims that Jesus is the sustainer of the universe. The creative Word that brought the universe into being also holds it in being moment by moment. The verb used here indicates that the writer has in mind something dynamic, not static. The Son is 'carrying along' all things. This is why He is untouchable, incomparable.

IN HIS HANDS

He carries not only the universe on His shoulders, but, as Colossians tells us, 'all things that pertain to life'. He is in charge and is reigning over space and time, past, present and future – everything is in His hands. That means He carries our lives.

A little girl was taking her first train ride. Wide-eyed with fascination, she watched as telephone poles, cars, houses, and cows whizzed by. When the train approached a river, she became frightened.

'Oh, Mother,' she said, 'the train is going into the river!' But a bridge carried it across to the other side.

Later as the train sped towards a mountain, the child again voiced her fear:

'Mummy, we are going to run into that mountain!'

But a tunnel at its base let the speeding train pass through.

'Oh, Mother,' said the youngster, 'someone must have gone ahead and made a way for us.'

Christ has done just that. I'm learning daily for Him to carry the load of care, stress, pressure, demands of a sick, dying, heart-breaking world. God said, 'his burden shall be taken from him' (Isaiah 10:27). I love Jeremiah's words: 'Do not fear, O my servant ... do not be dismayed, I will save you from captivity … Have a rest and be at ease … no one shall make … (you) afraid' (Jeremiah 46:27).

Remember at this time of desperation God has the whole world on His shoulders. He is carrying me, I say it each day:

> *This is Your Work, O Lord,*
> *This is Your Day, O God.*
> *You are carrying me today O Lord,*
> *I am in Your Hand, You are in charge;*
> *You cannot fail.*
> *One with You is in a majority.*

We can see the sustaining work of Christ in the continued existence of the forces of nature and in the sustained pattern, the laws, which govern their inter-action. This is the way He normally 'bears along' the physical creation to its destined end. The picture here is not a mechanical one, of a piece of clockwork running 'on its own', but a more relational one of the Creator at work in the creation, energizing it by His power.

Jesus is also the Redeemer of creation. The universe we live in is a fallen, disordered and disfig-ured one. The Creator has done what is necessary to remove evil and its effects from His creation, and so to redeem and renew it.

In simple terms, the Impeccable Son of God is a Mighty God – and we must let Him carry us.

4

PREPARING FOR HIS PRESENCE

Whenever our Queen or a member of the Royal family visits an area or community, local officials co-operate to prepare for their coming. The motorcade route is carefully laid out, streets are prepared, repaired and all rubbish picked up. The townspeople who will meet with their Royal Highnesses all put on their best clothes. The finery, the colour, the flags waving, the offices, auditoriums and businesses all decorated – the best is done to give them the kind of welcome their special position deserves.

If our Monarch merits such thorough prepara-tions, certainly the Lord of the universe deserves far more?

John the Baptist was given the task of crying in the wilderness: 'Prepare the way of the Lord, make his paths straight' (Luke 3:4). Luke 3:11–14 details the practical ways of preparation he advocated: '"He who has give to him who has not ... and he who has food give to him who has nothing to eat ... " The tax collectors came to be baptized and asked, "What shall we do then?" John said to them, "Collect no more than what is due, do not defraud the people ..." Likewise the soldiers came to him and asked, "What shall we do then?" He replied, "Do not intimidate anyone or accuse falsely any, do not exact dishonestly money from them, be content with the wages you have!"'

Isaiah had urged people to prepare for God's coming by the removal of spiritual obstacles (Isaiah 40:3–4):

Mountains of pride and abuse must be levelled.
Valleys of human need must be filled in.
Crooked immoral paths must be straightened.
Rough places or oppression and corruption must be smoothed out.

Let's look in turn at each of these obstacles to the way of the Lord and at how removing them makes us ready for Christ's transforming presence.

1 DEALING WITH PRIDE

The ancient verse goes:

Of all the many foes we meet,
  None so oft mislead our feet
And none betray us into sin
  Like the foes that dwell within.

We need to be saved from ourselves – our pride, our tempers, our selfishness, and our self-will. One of my friends who was proud of his self-will and ability to make money experienced reverses that set him back to where he was when he started. He told me that this happened, he is sure, because God wanted to deliver him from his pride.

I asked a Christian doctor friend of mine, who also runs a church, about a man in his fellowship, Ivan. I remembered him from when I had spoken there four years previously. He had been converted as a Roman

Catholic and he had been particularly bigoted, never knowing anything else in his life. But suddenly he met Jesus. He came from a little country where his religion dominated everyone. He became so anti his former religion, he went along one day and held the priest up against the church door threatening to clout him, because he had never ever told him about hell, and had let his relatives all die without assurance of Christ's redemption. He hit one priest and threatened a few others. But we had to tell him it was not the way, he had to show love, forgiveness, kindness, brotherhood, compassion for all God's people, show Christ was loving. Now He knew Him personally he must reveal it not by the fist but by a gentle, peaceful hand!

We soon found although mightily changed, he was still ruled by pride. A man who could have gone a long way became one moving from church to church feeling he knew it all, and it spoilt him.

Another man was fired from three good jobs before he realized that his worst enemy in each instance was not his boss, but himself – his own nasty temper.

A husband and wife were extremely preoccupied with their careers and with material things until they became foster parents for several boys. Only then were they delivered from their selfishness.

King Uzziah's pride brought him down. It killed him. We can all learn from this. We need to be saved from ourselves. Our pride, temper, selfishness, or self-will may be our worst enemy. Pride cuts off God's presence.

So how do we cure ourselves of pride? 'Let nothing be done through ... conceit, but ... let each esteem others better than himself' (Philippians 2:3). C. S. Lewis made this insightful comment: 'We say that people are proud of being rich, or clever, or good-looking, but they are not. They are proud of being richer, or cleverer, or better looking than others. If everyone else became equally rich, or clever, or good-looking, there would be nothing to be proud about.' Pride afflicts all of us, not just the rich and famous. It is our pride that causes us to feel hurt when we think someone has snubbed us, ignored us, or taken credit for something we did. Pride is behind our feelings of envy towards the person who is more successful than we are.

In his book, *Forever Triumphant*, F. J. Huegel wrote:

> Let us presume that I have had my feelings hurt. Just remember that more Christians go on the rocks, defeated, over the nasty little thing we call 'hurt feelings' than over the so-called great crises which test the very fibre of the soul. I have been slighted. I have not been given the place I feel I merit, or I have been treated inconsiderably, unjustly. Self has been wounded. As a result I have begun to sink. I am defeated, not by a monster but by a mere fly, and yet it is no less a devastating defeat to my spirit formerly free and rejoicing, I have sunk ... My step has become heavy, and my face now carries an unhappy, darkened look. I am plainly defeated.

Huegel then explained why that happens: 'Wounded pride did it. I looked at myself and took my eyes off Jesus.'

Do you feel self-sufficient? Are you easily hurt by others? Maybe it's time to get your focus off self and back on Jesus. That's a sure cure for pride. Samuel L. Brengle, a brilliant orator and highly successful pastor, was so burdened by the plight of the inner city poor that he resigned his church and joined the Salvation Army in London. Soon after being inducted, he was given the task of cleaning a pile of muddy boots. This was too much! Inwardly he rebelled. But then he thought about how Jesus washed the feet of His disciples. He asked the Lord for a servant spirit, cleaned the boots, and went on to a fruitful ministry among the disadvantaged.

This attitude does wonders. It frees us from the hurt feelings, animosities, jealousies, and resentment that cause us so much misery and cripple us spiritually. Ask Jesus to help you have a servant spirit. It will change your life.

This is how one young pastor dealt with his pride. The mother was paralysed and the son just sat around the house and ate. As a result, he gained so much weight that he couldn't stoop over to care for his feet. Two elderly Christian sisters who lived next door had compassion on the mother and came regularly to bathe her and to attend to her needs. But they couldn't help her son. Hearing about the need, the young pastor began stopping by to wash the son's feet and cut his toenails. The son would always heap on him abusive language, but the pastor kept coming back, proving that compassion persists in finding a way to help. Those smelly, old feet were a stench. He could easily have asked another believer to 'fill in for him', but no, he went personally – for months he did it. He was never the same again, his pride died.

O Lord you have searched me and known me ...
Such knowledge is too wonderful for me ...
Psalm 139:1,6

Two couples on vacation in England were driving along the shore of a large body of water. As they were discussing whether it was the English Channel or the Falmouth Estuary, they saw two women walking along the pavement.

'John, pull over there and I'll ask those ladies if this is the English Channel,' said Max. He rolled down the window and said to one of the women, 'Excuse me, ma'am, is that the English Channel?'

She glanced over her shoulder and said, 'Well, that's part of it.'

That woman's answer also applies to people. Like the English Channel, a large part of who we are lies unseen by others and even ourselves.

David was overwhelmed by the knowledge of God's all-knowing yet all-loving response to him. It created within him a desire to be pure before God in every part of his life (Psalm 139:23–24). And that's the kind of attitude we all need.

Your life is an open book to God – what does He read in you? What are you like privately? How do you treat others?

In the late 1700s, the manager of Baltimore's largest hotel refused lodging to a man dressed like a farmer because he thought this fellow's appearance would discredit his inn. So the man left. Later that evening, the innkeeper discovered that he had turned away none other than Thomas Jefferson! Immediately he sent a note to the famed patriot, asking him to come back and be his guest. Jefferson replied by instructing his messenger as follows: 'Tell him I have already engaged a room. I value his good intentions highly, but if he has no place for a dirty American farmer, he has none for the Vice-President of the United States.'

Likewise, the Lord is often pushed aside in our lives because we disregard needy believers of humble circumstances. We forget that Christ may be in the small child who needs attention, the exhausted wife who needs encouragement, or the frustrated labourer who needs recognition. He might be in the grieving grandmother or the struggling neighbour. Such individuals may seem to have little to offer, but if we show kindness to the 'least of these,' we are doing it to Christ.

3 A SMOOTH WAY

A minister called on a man whose wife was a faithful church member. He wanted to talk to him about his spiritual life. The man listened respectfully but said he wasn't ready to give his life to Jesus. Suddenly the man's wife, who was listening, placed her hands over her face and started to pray. She confessed to the Lord that she had been a poor example to her husband. As she prayed, tears began to stream down the husband's face and he dropped to his knees alongside her. That day he made a decision that changed his life.

Yes, we can make it difficult for others to come to Christ or to live fully for Him. Lying, cheating, angry words, bad language, and cruelty are obstacles that can cause others to stumble.

Let's get rid of the stones and rough places in our lives so that others will be able to follow a smooth pathway.

Christ died on the Cross to extend His love and grace to people of every race and social class. He 'shows no partiality' (Acts 10:34), and therefore He wants us to avoid discrimination towards others. Fawning over those who are rich or influential while being rude and indifferent to the poor or to those of another race is strongly condemned by God.

A deplorable incident occurred in the life of Mahatma Gandhi. He said in his autobiography that during his student days he was interested in the Bible. Deeply touched by reading the Gospels, he seriously considered converting to Christianity. The Christian faith seemed to offer the real solution to the caste system that was dividing the people of India. One Sunday he went to a church to see the minister and ask for instruction on the way of salvation and other Christian doctrines. But when he entered the sanctuary, the ushers refused him a seat and suggested that he go and worship with his own people. He left and never went back. 'If Christians have caste differences also,' he said to himself, 'I might as well remain a Hindu.'

Believer, weed from your heart the evil root of racial prejudice before it yields the same bitter fruit.

Lord, take away my prejudice,
Extend to me Your grace,
And help me show Your love to all,
No matter what their race.

4 EXORCIZING THE OPPRESSIVE

Many are bound by age-old traditions, religious ideas and customs, carnalities, out-of-date ideas, fears, cautions, small-mindedness.

In John 15:15 it says: 'I call you not servants ... '
There is a slave mentality towards God and a son
mentality, a servitude and sonship. We need to
move onward from followership to fellowship.
Augustine of Hippo said: 'There are many believers but few disciples.' We are seeing converts
to Christ come from simple trust to dedicated
service.

Jesus makes disclosures of His will and character
to the mature. The secrets of heaven, the mysteries of
the kingdom are revealed to His friends. Remember
how, in 1 Samuel 9:15, 'The Lord had told Samuel in
his ear'. The Lord draws close to His friends, we hear
messages of His love. 'The secret of the Lord is with
those who fear Him; and He will show them His
covenant' (Psalm 25:14).

As we obey we draw near – we walk in full discipleship, lose all inhibitions, all oppressions and
binding spirits, corruptions, dishonesties, selfishness
and greediness.

OBEY TODAY!

An advertisement for Ford cars showed a cartoon
of a man with a sign, 'THE WORLD WILL END
TOMORROW'. The other man stood around the
corner with another sign, 'THAT STILL GIVES
YOU ALL DAY TO SHOP AT YOUR FORD
DEALER YEAR-END CLEARANCE SALE ... !'

Delayed obedience is the brother of disobedience.
'Exhort one another daily, while it is called "Today",
lest any of you be hardened' (Hebrews 3:13).

To be adequately prepared for His presence, we must
see pride crushed, our inner self filled in, truly prac-
tising the Christ-life, and eliminating all oppressive-

40

ness in our living. Then we must cap it with His Kingship in us.

We must be prepared to experience the loss of all things for the supremacy of Christ. 'I count all things loss,' wrote St Paul, 'for the excellency of the knowledge ... of knowing Jesus Christ the Lord' (Philippians 3:7–8). The Amplified Bible has it: 'All things are nothing compared with the priceless privilege of knowing Jesus'.

Prepare yourself for the priceless privilege of His presence!

5

I LEARN FROM JESUS HOW EASY IT IS

It was as a young lad of 17 years of age in the third row of the cinema in the centre of Bristol, that I first experienced the personal cleansing of Jesus for my sin. To keep a praising heart, to keep above the waves of a desperate, anxious, transgression-stressed age, with which I am closely entwined, having a Gospel ministry and calling, costs something in effort, prayer watching, and as I've learned continuous cleansing is needed.

The story goes of a church down hard on its heels, the smallish congregation had little finance and although everyone gave generously, most were poor. God met them in an unusual way. Above the altar of this traditional church was a beautiful, carved, wooden structure. It was high up, and dirt, pollution and layers upon layers of dust had covered it over to this generation. Some workmen had to get up there to do an urgent job, and noticed it. After some cleaning, this magnificent carving came to light. It was unfixed and brought down. Experts valued it, and it was eventually sold for a million pounds. It's now a very rich little church!

How years of tradition, centuries of ritual, decades of ceremony and paraphernalia has hidden the true message from believers' hearts! Theology and dogma have replaced heart religion. Humanism and Psychology have replaced true guidance from the Holy

Spirit. Will-power, mind creation and human effort have replaced true spirituality.

I have learned from God it is easy, there is no need for a substitute. It's all in His Word, a constant cleansing is all that is needed to know and keep the vision of Him, His beauty and His magnificence clear before us.

ROOM SERVICE

Preaching and praying for the many desperate sick people, it was 1.30 a.m. when I finally climbed into bed. I slept so soundly that I did not notice my host coming quietly into my room with a nice, hot, English breakfast. Bacon, eggs, toast, tomatoes, sausage, plus cereal, hot milk and brewed tea. I awoke oblivious of his presence and shouted my usual good morning welcome to the day: 'PRAISE THE LORD!' He got such a fright, that suddenly the tray dropped out of his hand, milk spilt all over the eggs and bacon, the toast dropped into the cereal, the tea all over the tray.

He looked at the mess and smilingly inquired, 'Do you always greet the morning like that?' I gave another burst, 'PRAISE THE LORD ... JESUS IS ALIVE!'

He is such a reality to me I love Him. He is my life and breath, He lifted me. With no confidence in life, no hope, no peace, no future, lost and futile, Jesus lifted me, and gives me His daily presence. 'Closer is He than breathing, nearer than hands or feet ... '

But I have to be washed through and through first, by the Living God daily to keep that virtuous, worshipping, loving heart.

I like Heber's words in his hymn:

Holy, Holy, Holy! Though the darkness hide
Thee,
Though the eye of sinful man Thy glory may
not see;
Only Thou art holy – there is none beside Thee
Perfect in power, in love, and purity.

God's awesome presence convicts the sinner and comforts the saint.

TOO BEAUTIFUL TO BEAR

Woe is me, for I am undone! ... for my eyes have seen the King, the Lord of hosts.
Isaiah 6:5

Located about four miles west of New Mexico's Carlsbad Caverns is Lechuguilla Cave, a national treasure. Explorers who have descended deep into its interior describe a wonderland whose beauty is beyond almost anything they have ever seen.

Detroit Free Press writer Kelley Lewis quotes a geologist as saying, 'Everything is alien ... I've been in caves that are so beautiful that you just have to leave. You just can't take it.' Apparently that's how the explorers felt about Lechuguilla Cave.

Their experience gives us a clue to the problem we have with understanding a Holy God. He is so arrayed in splendour, so pure in His goodness, and so beautiful in His character that our sin-darkened eyes cannot bear to look on Him. We cannot endure His glory.

We need to examine our own history as Christian

believers. How many Christians today are guilty of the same sin? Too often our Christianity is in our mouths and not in our minds. Which of us cannot identify with the words of the apostle Paul who said, 'For the good that I will to do, I do not do; but the evil I will not to do, that I practise' (Romans 7:19).

Often the outsider can see through our facades; he calls it hypocrisy. He has heard the stories of Christian churches that have been divided by anger and hatred. He knows how some of the Sunday morning faithful spend Saturday night!

Myron Augsburger has written:

> Sin is the perversion of the good; it is the cheaper form of something better. Sin is not just things that we have done; rather, it is a perversion at the very core of our being that causes us to deify self and demand our own way. In this self-centredness, we are persons formed in our own image, rather than what we were created to be – persons created in God's image.
>
> The answer to our sin is not simply restitution for a few bad things that we have done. The answer is to turn to God and open ourselves to Him. All sin is ultimately against God.

We must never grow complacent about sin or simply say, 'Oh well, everyone else is doing it too.' The Bible commands: 'But just as He who called you is holy, so be holy in all you do' (1 Peter 1:15). It also tells us that there is forgiveness and new life when we repent and confess our sins to Christ. Man may whitewash sin, but only Jesus can wash it white.

In a story about the early mountain people, they used to have a wooden cradle with slatted sides to put their laundry in. The cradle was placed crossways in a rushing creek, and as the water flowed through the slats, the laundry was continuously cleansed. This was probably the first automatic washing machine in North Carolina. One day a bootlegger in that area was converted. When he was taken down to the stream to be baptized, he asked if he could please be put crossways to the current so that he would 'get washed the cleaner'!

When sin and failure come into our lives, as they most certainly will, we still have the wonderful promise that, 'the blood of Jesus, his Son, purifies us from all sin' (1 John 1:7). Jesus loves us too much to let us remain as we are.

In his book, *Ephesians: Key Words of the Inner Life*, F. B. Meyer observed that God 'is only too ready to forgive':

As the hungry sea frets down the line of cliff to find an opening through which to pour itself, and seethes and sobs until it finds room, so does the love of God wait impatiently outside our hearts till we open to it in confession and repentance. Then God forgives, not meagrely or stintingly, but royally, gracefully, abundantly. His forgiveness is worthy of Himself, proportioned to the wealth of His glorious being, and according to the riches of His grace. He does more than forgive; He 'remembers no more'. He does more than forget: He sets the joybells ringing ... He does more than this: He insets the scars of our sins with jewels – where sin abounded, His grace abounds much more – and all because of the Blood that has set free this wealth of mercy.

Thank God for His forgiving grace!

Through this cleansing there is a closeness to God. All the things that spoil us come to the fore, there is a new passion for holiness; so that evil habits, false beliefs, occult practices, bitterness, misery, fear, doubts, unsound doctrine all go 'by the board'! We are welcomed back to His close family, we have a new sense of direct, divine participation in our lives. God's love becomes close, incredible. The marvellous person of Jesus is a living daily reality and wonder to us.

LOOK STRAIGHT AHEAD

The story goes of the little child who had to go home alone at night, and to get to her house had to pass the cemetery. It was often dark as she passed that way. Was she not afraid, a friend asked her. She replied: 'I look straight ahead, I keep my eyes towards my home, then as I run, I sing and sing, I feel happy, I get through the darkness quicker and always get home safe.'

Sing, keep your eyes on your destination, look ahead, look to Jesus for hope, for cleansing. Jesus is at the Father's right hand, waiting to lift us, help us, cleanse us. So many believers talk weakness, see only their failure, their inadequacies. They talk like this: 'I am a weak worm, I'm not worthy. I was an adulterer,

I was a homosexual, I was a liar, I was a thief, I was corrupt, I was on drugs, my husband left me. Look at the life I've wasted. I've lost years, I'll never be strong in faith like others. Why did I do all that? I'm no good … ' This is not God-glorifying.

I've got good news for you – waste no more time looking at the past. Scripture tells us, 'Press towards the mark of the prize of the high calling.' For we have no sins when we are washed by Jesus Christ. We are clean in His sight, when we are washed in His blood. We are strong when we are washed. We have His righteousness when we are made clean through His sacrifice.

LET THE WEAK SAY I AM STRONG

Jesus tasted death for everyone. He died with my sins upon Him – lost, dark, full of fear, guilty, vile, condemned, depressed. He comes to us with victory, giving us His righteousness. As we emphasize living in, understanding and seeking the righteousness of Christ, we shall glow in His glorious presence. The emphasis again and again must be on what He achieved at Calvary, the wounds, bruises, suffering of the Saviour. Paul reminds us, 'The preaching of the Cross is the power of God unto salvation'. But why the blood, sacrifice, punishment, pain, agony and shame of Golgotha? Why? Why? … Paul goes on: 'Because therein is the righteousness of God revealed'. How? By the Cross Christ has become our righteousness … in that truth lies His glory, His Presence!

For a long time the old-style church stood in a city neighbourhood, empty and abandoned. White paint peeled and dropped from its clapboard walls. The decaying church blended naturally into the whole area. Shop fronts were boarded up. An old school building was padlocked. Grim, unswept, forgotten – that's how it all looked. But one night a local who often drove through the dark neighbourhood was greatly surprised to see the old church ablaze with light. Parked cars lined the streets. The sound of music filled the air. What had been dead and abandoned had come to life.

I've seen people like that. For years they were dark and empty like that old church. They had the look of being Christian, but there was little inside except anger, selfishness, and pride. Then one day all was changed. Suddenly the darkness was gone. It was as if someone had turned on the lights and filled their lives with music. Do such changes surprise us? They shouldn't. God specializes in giving life to those who seem beyond hope.

God's Kingly rule begins in your life in revival. There is a fervent expectation, there is no morbid, formal, dull religious living. He gets closer and closer to you. He is always available, approachable, loving, careful, generous, wanting to hug you, wanting to enfold you in His arms and welcome you home!

This is what I found, this is what keeps me strong, this is what helps ease the burden, when Jesus washes me clean, refreshing me within. I trip up, I am hit hard, I stumble; but I pick myself up easily with His grace, because I've clear insight, I'm washed inside daily.

6

How to Get a Hunger for God

Good things are commencing to happen as the presence of the enthroned Christ increases amongst His people in parts of the UK and across Europe. It is small, but increasingly we find the character of Jesus becomes immensely attractive to us. From being so unlike Him, so far from His model, we become scared of hypocrisy, bored by the churches' blandness, ashamed of our powerlessness. The mighty, consuming, awe-striking presence sweeps all before it, I'm discovering.

Christ is All. As Richard Baxter said, 'If we can but teach Christ to our people, we teach them all.' We are getting back to health, as ailing believers wake up and focus on Christ the principal One! We are starting to live like Jesus – if so, Britain will soon be ours! As Count Zinzendorf cried, 'I have but one passion, 'tis He, only He (Jesus)'.

God is bringing revival to an ailing church, or raising up a new church. This is happening now – an extravagant love and feeling of God is present amongst us. We are engaged in a relentless pursuit of Him, as he rains down fire upon us. We have a new confidence in His supernatural Gospel. The promises have become real, living to us. We have a new status with Him. And as Paul wrote, 'We, who … reflect the Lord's glory, are being transformed into His likeness with ever increasing glory, which comes from the

Lord, who is the Spirit … !' (2 Corinthians 3:18). We are now crying hungrily with Jacob: 'I will not let you go unless you bless me (more) … ' (Genesis 32:26).

But how can you and indeed all believers have that hunger for God? Hunger for God requires us to seek God, to journey in faith. The Lord said to Moses, 'Why are you crying out to Me? Tell the Israelites to move on' (Exodus 14:15). Jesus commanded: 'Go out to the world with the Good News to all creation' (Mark 16:15). A forward movement with Him – the whole emphasis of God is on 'advance'. It is likened to a pilgrim journey – 'to the eternal city' (Hebrews 11:16). Hudson Taylor said: 'God is always advancing.' We are at fault if we fail to follow.

So what are the keys to this hunger? Here are 10 ways to get hungry for God and into His presence.

1 LAY ASIDE EVERY WEIGHT OF SIN

'Let us lay aside every weight and sin which so ensnares us … looking to Jesus, who endured the Cross and sat down at the right hand of God' (Hebrews 12:1–2).

During the 1992 general election campaign there was a party political broadcast which showed a film of two runners – one the defending Government of the day, the other the Opposition party, running neck and neck to the finishing line. Suddenly the opposition party took on a heavy weight marked 'increased taxes', the other got a few inches ahead, then took another weight marked 'increased local rates', then another, 'higher inflation'. Soon he was far behind and the other party had won clearly.

Many believers carry added weights on their run for God. There are all kinds of extra baggage which you may have incurred: unbiblical traditionalism, criticism of others, some uncleanness or bad habit, disobedience, doubts, lack of love, meanness with money, not paying tithes, gifts, failing to give liberally to God's work. And so on and on – the list could be endless.

Paul advised: 'Strip down, start running, no extra spiritual fat, no parasitic signs' (Hebrews 12:6). Remember: the Christian Life is a pilgrim journey, not a pleasure trip.

During his term as President of the United States, Lyndon Johnson was somewhat overweight. One day his wife challenged him with this blunt assertion: 'You can't run the country if you can't run yourself.' Respecting Mrs Johnson's wise observation, the President lost 23 pounds!

As believers in Christ, we are challenged by the author of Hebrews to rid ourselves of 'every load ... never quit, don't feel sorry for yourselves ... don't flag' (Hebrews 12:1,3–4). This includes disregarding anything that encumbers our spiritual effectiveness. By discipline and self-control, we must shed any habit, practice, or attitude that is hindering our spiritual welfare and service of the Lord. Such self-discipline is necessary if we are to 'run with endurance the race that is set before us' (Hebrews 12:1).

The way to achieve this self-control is to place ourselves under the Holy Spirit's control. Are there any sinful excesses in our lives? Do we need to lose some 'weight'? If so, it's time to exercise self-control by submitting ourselves to the Spirit's control. If your Christian Life is a drag – worldly weights may be to blame!

A vicar dedicating a child found the baby had exactly the same names as he had, he asked the parents: 'Why, do you want him to be like me one day – a parson?'

The mother replied, 'Oh no, he'll have to work for his living!'

It costs to yield! Jesus said, 'Not to do mine own will but yours'. He laid aside with no hesitation. He was great but laid aside his greatness. He was rich but became poor to make us rich.

The humility of God is beyond comprehension. Do not have self-will and prohibit Jesus from working in your life. Christ disciplined Himself for you, ever free but eternally bound – a paradox. No force compelled Him but the force of love for us. He was a model of self-denial. Putting on a human body to cross this world of pain, for our world's salvation at immense pain and suffering, He yielded. We are riveted to His Son, His love has bundled us up with Jesus, He has made a death-defying link with us, His children. Almighty, yet He reaches out to the alienated world.

> The Lowliness is seen in His compassion – be tender, devout as He,
> The tenderness of God is seen in the gentle Jesus – be kind as He,
> The wisdom of God is seen in the Teacher sent from God – learn from Him,
> The omnipotence of God is seen in His wonders, signs, and miracles today – receive them freely,
> The love of God is seen in a crucified Lord – take Him right into your heart and life now!

Surrender to the Holy Spirit. Say 'Yes' to His demands within your spirit and soul. Faith in the Holy Spirit produces a living link with the Father, it begets a greater hunger and desire after God. Faith then sees the potential behind the invisible. Such yielding is penetrating, it is positive, as it accepts the reality hidden in that appointment with the Spirit of God and then embraces the personality of the Holy Spirit with an external presence. Hunger and satisfaction are both the outcomes of yielding: you want more and more of God and from God.

3 DYING TO SELFISHNESS AND OBEYING HIM AT ANY COST

The Apostle Paul writes in Romans 8:12–13, 'We are debtors – not to live unto the flesh, for if you live according to the flesh, you will die, but if by the Spirit you put to death the deeds of the flesh, you will live.'

Crucify the flesh, fight it, keep in the Spirit, ask God to help you to conquer it. Get into the Word of God, again read, read and re-read whole passages. I've never known anyone ever defeated by the Devil again once they got into this Word day by day. I try to read or listen to on average 150 chapters a week. Resurrection power flows into you when you die to selfishness and the flesh. It's an ongoing process: God speaks, we listen and say 'Yes'.

As Christians, we face strong foes that would bring us into spiritual defeat. Our greatest enemy, however, lurks within. 'For from within ... proceed evil thoughts ... covetousness, wickedness, deceit' (Mark 7:21–22). Even though we have been born again, we are deeply aware of our inclination towards evil. In

Victor Hugo's story, 'Ninety-Three', a ship is caught in a storm. The frightened crew hear a terrible crashing sound below. Immediately the men know what it is: a cannon has broken loose and is crashing into the ship's side with every smashing blow of the sea! Two men, at the risk of their lives, manage to fasten it down again, for they know that the unfastened cannon is more dangerous than the raging storm. Hillery C. Price made this application: 'Many people ... are like that ship – their greatest danger areas lie within their own lives.'

When we are walking in our own way we are actually running from the Lord. The cost of obedience is nothing compared with the cost of disobedience. God does not demand of us success, but obedience. Obedience belongs to us; results belong to God.

The way of obedience is the way of blessing – and the way to increase your appetite for God.

4 LIVE IN THE REALM OF THE SPIRIT

Someone once said, 'Your knees will not knock if you kneel on them.' We must be rid of pride, be broken on our faces before God. Swallowing your pride won't give you indigestion; it will change you. Rely on God, die to human reliability, walk in the realm of the Holy Spirit.

Kathryn Kuhlman said, 'I die a thousand deaths before going on stage.' I always get very nervous on a first night of a crusade. My staff tell me that the place is packed, the press and media are present, extra chairs are being found and many sick and badly crippled people in wheelchairs are present. I feel the immense need and challenge and responsibility. But living in the Spirit lifts me above everything – I don't see the blind, the dying children – I look beyond and see the sky full of the armies of God and the powers of heaven. I see those that are for us not the impossibilities against us.

Only the Holy Spirit can give you that vision and insight, and, living in prayer we live in the Holy Spirit. If we appreciate Him, talk to Him, welcome Him and do not grieve Him. The more we are encouraging ourselves in spiritual fellowship with the Spirit of God, the hungrier we get for more.

5 YIELD TO GOD FOR THE IMPOSSIBLE

As He calls you to do bigger things for Him, you must say 'Yes' – don't question Him. Do the small task, yield to do the impossible. As you enjoy working for Him, you hunger to do more. But it means self-surrender.

There is an old Chinese story of two men walking along the riverside one day, when suddenly there is a cry from an anxious voice. A man is in the river struggling, and it is quite clear he is drowning. One Chinaman said to the other, 'I cannot help him, I cannot swim, but you are a strong swimmer!' The other said nothing about the drowning man, but just continued with his original conversation!

The drowning man went down the first time, then came up screaming. The man on the bank who could not swim looked much concerned – saying to his friend, 'Are you not going to save him?' The other man ignored the drowning man and his plea and just went on walking and talking.

The man in the river came up screaming a second

time, but still there was no response from the strong swimmer on the bank. As he went down for the third time, suddenly the man on the bank threw off his garment and dived in. He pulled the drowning man to the surface and soon had him up on the bank, pumping water from his lungs. Before long he was sitting up recovering.

The man who had watched everything said to the life-saver, 'Why did you leave it till the very last second before saving him?' And the man replied, 'I waited till he stopped struggling.'

God is waiting for our self-surrender, for us to stop fighting, stop struggling, stop arguing with Him. There is no democracy in the Kingdom of God. It is total authoritarianism. God rules. Christ rules. The Holy Spirit dictates to us. 'Our sole authority for spiritual direction is the Holy Scripture,' said John Wycliffe. He speaks, He commands, He demands.

I was once in a great meeting with Corrie Ten Boom. She only spoke for a few minutes and she virtually said the same thing over and over again, but she left something behind deep in the hearts – perhaps more than those who preached for two hours! She kept saying, in her quiet Dutch voice, 'There is only one way forward with the Master – surrender, surrender, surrender ... '

6 HUNGER FOR GOD IS BORN
IN A TIME OF MUCH LOVE

Paul wrote to the church at Thessalonica: 'May the Lord make your love to grow and overflow towards each other, and to everyone else, just as our love does to you. This will result in your hearts being made strong, sinless, and holy by God our Father' (1 Thessalonians 3:12–13). No wonder this church in Greece was so strong! Love was their hallmark.

As I keep a clear vision before me – full of God's love – it gives me a penetrating hunger after the Living God.

In that marvellous children's classic, *Wind in the Willows*, Kenneth Grahame records a conversation between Mole and Rat. Mole had never seen a river before and as he looks out on the swirling waters exclaims:

'Is this a river?'
'Yes, this is the river.'
'You really live on it.'
'It's my world, I want no other way, I live by it, with it, on it, and in it!'

So as believers we must live by Christ, with Christ, on Christ, and in Christ. He is our vision. Tozer has said: 'We have become so engrossed in the work of the Lord, that we have forgotten the Lord of the work!' Let us gain a new vision and go in Godly love on a Holy Crusade for a pure Church, turning away from the worldliness that has become almost epidemic amongst evangelical people. Let us turn to the true vision of dynamic, perfect love and holiness.

What happens when a ten-year-old girl ties a note to a helium-filled balloon and sends it on its way to heaven? According to *Detroit Free Press* writer, Bob Greene, a grieving Illinois girl named Sarah sent such a letter to her grandfather, who had died before she could have one last visit with him. The letter was addressed 'To Grandpa Bernie, in Heaven Up High.'

It represented a little girl's expression of love, and her hope that somehow Grandpa would hear.

Two months passed, and a letter arrived addressed to Sarah. It began, 'Your letter to Grandpa Bernie apparently reached its destination and was read by him. I understand they can't keep material things up there, so it drifted back to Earth. They just keep thoughts, memories, love, and things like that.'

If we are moved by this girl's love for her grandpa, what about those we love who are still living? Death and eternity have a way of putting things in perspective. Paul, in his first letter to the Thessalonians, wrote as one who knew the lasting value of relationships. He expressed his deep love and encouraged them to increase in their love for one another. The love we give is the only love we keep, and this makes us spiritually hungry!

7 GO ON REPENTING

To keep hungry and satisfied in His presence, keep repenting. Some turn off on a detour, even some of God's finest people give up or fade away or get weak and discouraged, the fire burns out.

In one section of John Bunyan's *Pilgrim's Progress*, Christian and Hopeful are walking the King's Highway to the Celestial City. The path, once smooth and easy, becomes rough and hard. Then they come to an attractive place called Bypath Meadow. They climb over a fence into the meadow and the new path becomes easy again. But only for a time.

Soon the new path becomes rugged and steep. A terrible storm breaks overhead. Exhausted by the effort to continue, Christian and Hopeful lie down and fall asleep. Suddenly they are awakened by the owner of the meadow, the Giant of Despair, who drags them to Doubting Castle and throws them into a dungeon where he taunts them, beats them, and starves them. Hurt and confused, they despair.

Finally Christian and Hopeful begin to pray. Then Christian remembers that he is carrying in his pocket a key called Promise. Quickly he uses it to open the doors of the dungeon, and then the gate of the castle. Freedom! Soon they are on the King's Highway again.

Are you doubting? Filled with despair? Perhaps somewhere along the line you chose to leave God's will to enter some pleasurable bypath.

Genuine repentance is painful. It hurts our pride and wounds our ego. But it's a needful and healing hurt. The Baouli people of West Africa describe repentance this way, 'It hurts so much I want to quit it.' That's why it comes so hard.

God's desire is to share Himself with us: 'My presence shall go with you, and I will give you peace' (Exodus 33:14). He spoke these words, 'I am the Lord your God who brought you out of the land of slavery' (Exodus 20:2). He called us, chose us, passed millions by to reach out to us, and adopted us. 'To all who received Him, to them gave He the might to become children of God' (John 1:12). He approached us, to have fellowship with us – aliens, sinners, unworthy, blasphemers. He spoke to us from heaven.

Many of us know and rejoice in the truth of 1 John 1:9, 'If we admit our sins – make a clean breast of them – he won't let us down, He'll be true – He'll forgive … and purge all our wrongdoing.' But how often do we identify with and express sorrow for the sins of others? We may not be responsible for their wicked deeds, but we are members of the same human family, and we have within us the potential to commit the same sins others do, even those sins that shock us. Nehemiah did not hesitate to align himself with the iniquities of his fellow countrymen. He prayed, 'Both my father's house and I have sinned. We have acted very corruptly against You.' Such is the humility we need in order to pray for others in the right way. In this is love, and in caring for others our own thirsting and hunger for Jesus is partly met.

Repent of all sins. Go on repenting, seven days a week for God. Nothing can stop us knowing mightily His presence, nothing can stop us pulling down the walls of Jericho, if we are living and abiding in Him.

Men and women sold out for Jesus. With the anointing of His presence I'm like a superman, without it I'm a wimp. With the Holy Spirit, I'm like a man from another world.

8 GOD CALLS A PURE PEOPLE

A wet night, a friend of mine, his car lights very dim, got out in the pouring rain and cleaned the head lamps. Soon they were beaming brightly.

The dirt and soil of sin have got between us and our Lord. He calls for us to be whiter than white. 'Who is this who will climb the hill of the Lord? He that hath clean hands and a pure heart' (Psalm 24:4).

Man is seeking desperate remedies. He's in a desperate situation, he's looking for supernatural men and women in the Church. Find a hurt, heal it; find a need, meet it. A pure people are a powerful people. Jesus came into the cities in His day and brought hope, He brought life into the city of the dead. We have unbroken power from the times of the apostles, and its foundation is purity.

Sin quenches spiritual desire to know His presence. Psalm 34:16: 'The face of the Lord is against those who do evil, to cut off their remembrance on the earth.' In contrast, 'The eyes of the Lord are open to the righteous, His ears open to their cries ... the righteous cry out and the Lord hears them ... the Lord is near to those who have a broken heart and saves such' (Psalm 34:15,17–18).

'All power is given to us in heaven and earth', and the greatest power in the world is THE WORD OF GOD. Through it sin can be eradicated, our greatest enemy can be defeated. Don't let inward sin quench you and lose His presence. It's time to give the Devil misery. It's time to give the Devil a hard time. It's time to set hell in shambles.

Jesus came to arrest the corrosion of sin and to reach starving souls. The Devil has no right to your children or grandchildren, he has no right to your home and your church, no right to your wallet, to your job or business. We are damaging the Devil's kingdom, God is shaking towns. GOD WANTS YOU TO BE HUNGRY FOR HIS POWER AND MIRACLES.

9 DESIRE TO BE PERFECT –
AND YOU WILL BE HUNGRY

Isaiah proclaimed that the hungry people shall be called 'the holy people', and 'the Lord's redeemed', and 'the city God has blessed'. In 1 Corinthians

6:9–11, Paul writes: 'Don't fool yourselves, those who live immoral lives ... will have no share in the Kingdom of God ... There was a time when some of you were just like that, but now your sins have been washed away, and you are set apart for God, and He has accepted you because of what the Lord Jesus Christ has done for you.'

A man fell over a cliff. He was drunk, but he managed to catch hold of a tree and was swinging from it in the pitch darkness. He shouted and called for help, but no one could hear the old drunk. Finally he thought he had better pray, and he called, 'O God help me, help me.' No answer. Then again, 'O God help me, save me!' Then a voice came, 'Turn loose, let go!'

In the deep darkness he could see nothing, and thought, 'That's not a good idea.' So he called out again, 'Is there anyone else up there?' Finally when he did let go, he fell two feet and was safe.

We don't like what we hear, we often will not listen. But God's advice and guidance is always best! Obey Him – hunger after being holy – desire to be like Jesus.

Not long before Christmas, a boy of eight entered the lingerie department of a well-known store. Bashfully, he told the assistant he wanted to buy a gift for his mother – an underskirt. The assistant asked her size but the boy didn't know. The assistant asked him to describe her. Was she fat, thin, tall or what?

'Well,' said the youngster, 'she's just about perfect.' So the assistant chose a size 12, and off he went happily.

On Monday, his mother came to the store to exchange the gift for a size 16, but after the assistant told her what her son had said, she left the store walking on air!

Aim at perfection – this will make you famished for God and his ways.

10 FINALLY – PRAY EARNESTLY

To be truly hungry for God, you must shake off apathy, be earnest, seek his ways – with all of your heart.

While waiting for the teller at a bank counter in Liverpool, England, Evangelist Charles Alexander picked up a pen and began to write on a pad of paper. Two words had gripped his heart: *pray through*. So he wrote them over and over until the paper was filled from top to bottom.

When the teller returned to the window, the preacher transacted his business and left. The next day, a friend visited Alexander to tell him a striking story.

A businessman had come into the bank shortly after Alexander had left. He was discouraged and weighed down with financial troubles. As he began to do his banking at the same counter, he noticed the pad with its long columns of *pray through*. When he learned from the teller that Charles Alexander had printed those words, he exclaimed: 'That is the very message I need! I have tried to *worry through* in my own strength, and have only mentioned my troubles to God. Now, I am going to *pray through* until I get light.'

James said of Elijah that 'he prayed earnestly'. Our heavenly Father waits to hear fervent, earnest, persistent prayer from us rather than feeble, apathetic requests. Yes, Pray Through! In the words of Hebrews

4:16, 'Let us come boldly to the throne of grace', or in a modern English rendering: 'Let's walk right up to Him and get what He is so ready to give'!

Howard Hendricks told of a new Christian who was attending his first prayer meeting and was afraid to pray aloud because he couldn't do it like the others. After some encouragement, he stood and said, 'Lord, this is Jim. I'm the one that met You last Thursday night. Forgive me, Lord, because I can't say it the way the rest of these people do, but I want to tell You the best I know how: I love You. Amen.' Hendricks said that man's simple prayer ignited the prayer meeting. HE WAS HUNGRY FOR HIS SAVIOUR!

Do all these things: lay aside every weight of sin; yield to the Holy Spirit; obey at all costs and die to selfishness; live in the realm of the Spirit; yield to God for the impossible; share much in His love; go on repenting; become pure; desire to be holy, and pray earnestly – be violent and desperate for the glory of God to meet you. If you do practise this you will be both hungry and gloriously thrilled and satisfied, and sail through life like a bird!

7

ACCESS TO THE KING AT ALL TIMES

I was travelling on a plane to a preaching appointment in Europe a few years ago. Sitting opposite me, with one empty seat between us, was a smart lady in her early forties. When the meal came round she passed the tray to me from the stewardess, commenting that she did not eat cheese. Would I like her portion as an extra? As I was slimming, I refused politely. She struck up a conversation from then on, asking me which company I owned, or worked for.

'Trinity,' I quietly replied.

She looked up, interested, 'I've never heard of them. What are they into … ?'

'Everything.'

'Telecommunications, electronics, translation … ?'

'All of it and more … it's endless,' I added.

'Are they big?'

'Massive – the very largest.'

'That's strange, I've never heard of them. Are they a new company?'

'Old as the hills, but ever new in its products!'

'What are their assets?'

'Incalculable. Billions upon billions, beyond all estimations … '

'This is fascinating. How many do they employ and how many countries?'

'Every nation in the world. Over 200 lands, at least one billion customers.'

'How many directors?'

'Only three.'

'You say there are only three in control?'

'Absolutely, they are more than adequate.'

'Who are the three?'

Then came the crunch, as I cheerily added: 'FATHER, SON AND HOLY SPIRIT.'

She nearly fell off her seat! She was so hot and flustered not knowing if I was a fanatic or an angel. But the conversation continued on a personal basis, she admitting her failures in life. Although a director in her firm, her career had cost her love, marriage, a broken heart, loneliness, sadness and guilt. She had money, plenty of this world's accumulations, but had lost hope, faith and confidence.

But she warmed up and joy came to her as I told her the glad tidings, that Christ was the glorious forgiver, the Kingdom was only a step away, a thrilling adventure lay at her heart's door.

As she went down the steps of the plane, I could see a new step, a new hope beginning. The Triune God was present on that aircraft. Christ was present. God the Father was at work at 30,000 feet! I had immediate access above the clouds at 750 miles per hour! Through His personal, glorious, lovely Name, all power, communication, revelation and life flowed into the airline cabin!

ACCESS

We are first on His heart, we have entrance before Him at all times. He called us, chose us, adopted us. 'You are among those who are called to belong to Christ' (Romans 1:6). 'To all who received Him, to them gave He the power to become the children of God' (John 1:12).

He approached us to have fellowship with us sinners. He spoke to us from heaven. He offered us mercy contrary to our deep demerits. He gave us a new heart, He gave us a changed being, He made us penitent believers.'He is able to save for all time, those who draw near to Him' (Hebrews 7:25). He has offered us a close friendship. Jesus says in John 15:14: 'You are My friends if you do whatever I command you.'

Friends of Jesus – what an offer! A close relationship, with dignity. He lifted us like beggars from the dung hill to put us among princes and princesses. Our joys are doubled, cares are halved, secrets shared, prayer becomes a holy dialogue instead of a pompous monologue. The Bible becomes a new book because we are acquainted with the Author. We discover that in temptation we have a powerful ally, in trouble a source of relief, in distress a shoulder to weep on. His friendship banishes loneliness, defies despair, makes life more liveable and enjoyable.

With Jesus close at hand, a friend of His, we face life's grim battles and win through. His Word will guide, His will our government, His work our grand activity. If our hearts are His ... His heart is ours.

It is settled, eternity has planned it,
It is sure, for God will help you perfect it,
It is a design duty must despatch,
Jesus followed a way that led to Calvary,
A Cross of shame, a cup of suffering,
He rode a chariot of grief that we may be swept
along on the chariots of God,

He bore our sin to load us with benefits.
An upward and forward urge in Christ draws us
on to greater heights in Him.
We have access, authority, action.

Access – *immediate* access. To mention the Name of
Jesus opens the pearly gate. The Name of Jesus is
more than a sound or an air-wave but rather it
defines the personality of Jesus as a personal Saviour,
it declares the position of Jesus as supreme. The suffi-
ciency of His divinity is in His Name, Jesus Christ,
Potentate of all time.

One of Moody's brothers sought to get admission
to one of his rallies, but in vain: it was so crowded he
could not get in. So he sent a message in: 'Tell him his
brother is outside.' Moody called him in, and gave
him a seat on the platform. The name of Moody
opened the door into the very centre of things, used
by his brother it opened the door. So with us, we have
access to the Father through the Name of Jesus – the
key to open heaven's portals.

AUTHORITY

Intimate friends of Jesus will know His mind, sense
His desire, respond to His Spirit, ask for those things
that glorify God, extend His kingdom, and enable
His Spirit to work. This produces results. In such a
context it is all powerful, 'in Thy Name,' means
according to His wishes, temperament and character.

Obedience in prayer brings fruit. I've learned to
instantly obey God: don't question, don't argue it
out, go quickly in obedience to be blessed.

A man was on his way to a big business deal, a big

order. Suddenly a voice said, 'Turn off at the next exit.'

'But Lord I can't, in a few minutes I've got to get this big money deal.'

'Turn at the next exit.'

He obeyed with an aggravated sigh. Soon he turned into a café forecourt and sat there for 10 minutes.

'I've lost that order, okay?'

Then he saw the depressed face of a man sitting in the window of the cafe. He ran in, ordered tea, talked to him, prayed and led him to Jesus and gave him some money. That man was in trouble, but he never looked back from that day. He was saved from suicide and went on to become a giant of faith. The businessman drove on and arrived late for his appointment, but so did his contact. The man gave him double the order he had expected! 'HE WHO HONOURS GOD – GOD WILL HONOUR.'

A man had money in stocks and shares, he had a top price for his company's land, it was going up and up, everything looked fine. That day he heard a voice saying, 'Sell immediately.' The man asked top men in stocks and they all said, 'It's crazy to sell now, hang on.' Everyone told him the same. The voice came rapidly, 'Sell, don't delay.'

He sold and got an excellent price. Others thought him mad, but the following day the bottom fell out of the market. There was a big collapse in shares, everyone lost millions, but he was tops!

LISTEN TO GOD. One old Pentecostal Preacher used to say, 'Always be half a step behind God, never in front, but always be quick to do what He tells you.' Sell out to the Word of God, fill yourself with the Word, it's the Word that produces fruit.

Jesus says, in John 15:16, 'I have chosen you and ordained you'. We have no right to question His choice; all His servants are hand-picked. The call has two sides: the call is in the emergent present, it has a request and a response. Jesus says, 'Will you?' We must say 'I will.' He proposes it – we perpetuate it. A compelling urge, a commission to go, forward looking plans, prospect-directed energy, progress-making action; ordained mission in Christ.

The sign of obedience is fruit, an important end, not just character but achievement. The fruit of the apostle is well-founded churches. The fruit of the prophet is edifying directives, of an evangelist, sound conversions, fruit of a teacher sound doctrine, fruit of a pastor a satisfying and growing flock. When each works by the will of God there are abiding results. We must have an *implemented* ministry, we must bear fruit. Jesus said: 'I put you into the world to bear fruit … that won't spoil' (John 15:16).

ACTION

There is endless talk in Britain: conferences, re-structuring, setting up new hierarchies in the Church, discussion groups, new presidents, superintendents, fresh systems, talk, talk, talk … Nothing but words, words and more words, but no power – few who can go and do it.

The blood of perishing millions is on our hands! We have only stifled the great commission while millions are dragged into outer darkness. I can hear the screams of the helpless multitudes pierce my ears. CRY OUT FROM YOUR HEARTS, REPENT,

THAT YOU HAVE NOT WON SOULS. Earnestly desire to reach unregenerate peoples. If we miss this call, this command, we will have less and less of His joy, prosperity, blessing, miracles, power, success. The dam is about to break. The flood has begun – God is up to something.

WE MUST BE FRUITFUL. Fruit reveals a consecrated saint, one made chaste by the chastenings of the Almighty, one who has been pruned of useless verbiage, whose flow of life has been directed in profitable channels, not wasting energy on profitless, fleshly pursuits. His ambition, endeavour and achievement is to see much fruit. Our delight is to please Him. A wise son makes for a glad father, a mature Christian pleases our heavenly Father: it shows the sacrifice of the Son has met its destined end, and is not dissipated as we show much fruit.

Fruitfulness is linked to discipleship, for in bearing fruit we reveal the marks of a disciple. *Matahase* (Greek for disciple) means 'an apprentice to a trade' – one who imitated the master craftsman. He learns by seeing the tradesman at work, following his ways, giving himself wholly to the master designer. His experience, creations, powers of know-how, wisdom, delicate, compassionate, expert, perfect touch gradually becomes his own. 'Purge me of self, O Lord, that I may bring forth much fruit for you.'

Satan is about to be routed, Jesus is in the control room. Armchair Christians have no fire or passion. The tempo must increase, we are called to share the spoils of Satan, we are to fill the whole earth with the praises of God. We must pierce the kingdom of darkness with the kingdom of light. 'Our help cometh from the Lord', who 'maketh a way where there is no way'.

72

Tap the limitless power of prayer. Don't be paralysed by inaction like the old law dating back 70 years in New England, USA, which says: 'When two vehicles meet at an intersection neither shall move till the other is past.' Some are paralysed by their forms, rituals, traditions, and denominations.

The Body Of Christ must deliver the people from their bondage. It's the *body* that will deliver the kingdom. I often say to congregations: 'I brought my body here today to deliver the message, I didn't leave it behind.' The body must deliver the message – don't get sidetracked by the obscure, the side issues. This is the most thrilling day ever. God wants to give you a great harvest, but the Holy Spirit works best where He is welcomed.

8

LAY HOLD OF GOD'S POWER

We were made by God to be like Christ. He wants to overflow our life. You can soon tell a man or a woman who is 'leaking with God's power and presence'. As a friend said, 'It is what spills out of you when you are bumped that shows what is in you.' A Christ-like person is not the one who is always telling you that he is! He or she is the one who under pressure and trial, when shaken, is still full of the grace and glory of the Master. Job experienced this, 'He prays to God and finds favour with Him, he sees His face and shouts for joy. He is restored by God to his righteous state' (Job 33:26). Are you in that righteous state? Have you truly died to the flesh?

A reporter once asked me, 'How many true Christians are there left in the UK?' He had quoted 1.5 million born again ones, plus millions of others, etc. I utterly shocked him when I said, 'Not more than 200 real Christians.' I meant those who had really died. It caused a great controversy, but I sincerely believe few have yet died. John Wesley in his day realized the same, when he stated at the commencement of his ministry: 'Give me twelve men who hate nothing more than sin, and love no one more than God, and I will take England over for Christ.' He very nearly did it after 50 years of preaching, with his tiny band. It costs!

Are you so filled in your heart with God's presence

that there is no room left for anything that does not honour God? Does your life so reflect the holy nature of the Lord who has called you to be like Him? This sin-weary generation waits for deeds of sanctified living – the greatest force in the world are those dead to the flesh, the world, the old life, full of God's undying love, marching out in His purity and presence.

TAKE A QUANTITY!

A young agnostic was having an argument with a minister and tried to put him on the spot by asking: 'How do you reconcile Matthew's version of Jesus' words, "Are not two sparrows sold for a penny?" with Luke's "Are not five sparrows sold for two pennies?"'

Quick as a flash, the minister replied: 'Because you get them cheaper if you take a quantity!'

We can minister as preachers for a lifetime, believers can strive, work, sweat, labour for years and years and achieve very, very little. It's cheaper by taking a quantity. It's far easier by giving yourself over to Him, let Jesus have it all. Let Jesus take every hard time, every attack, every sorrow, every heartache, every debt, every weight. Give it all to him. Life is easier, totally successful, prosperous, victorious when Jesus has it in His hands. Give it all to Him, in quantity, entirely, 100 per cent, all the way. Say, 'Take it all Jesus, I'm in Your hands, whatever the future holds I'm in Your hands.' Cry till this old life dies away inside of you.

Tozer, a remarkable 'prophet', wrote many articles, some books, but few verses. This man who walked with God, was finally turned away from most Bible camps by his evangelical colleagues and contemporaries, due to his strong preaching on crucifying the old life. I love three of the small number of verses this outstanding holy man did pen.

Born to endure the thorns, the rod,
The shameful wounds for our salvation.
Our sins, our woes come all before us,
We have no friend, no friend but Thee;
O spread Thy saving mantle o'er us,
And set our mourning spirits free.

Word of the Father! Hear our prayer!
Send far the evil tempter from us,
And make these souls Thy tender care
Lest sin and Satan overcome us.
O conquering Christ! Deep hell, despairing,
Must bow and own Thy right to reign,

Out of the depths do I cry,
O God, to Thee!
Hide now Thy face from my sin!
Fountains of tears flow in vain;
So dark the stain
Tears cannot wash it away.
Bearing the shame in my heart;
Broken with anguish I mourn all the day.

WE MUST HAVE OUR OWN WAY

God's people make it so hard for themselves. There is cost, but when we are in God's hands He leads the way, takes the initiative, gives divine inspiration and instruction. We no longer need to strive in the flesh; it is not human effort but Godly powers that carry the strain. Jesus said, 'My yoke is easy, My burden light' (Matthew 11:30). James declared, 'Wisdom from above is easy' (James 3:17). Again, 'Knowledge is easy to him that understands' (Proverbs 14:6). But we want it our way.

A five-year-old girl prayed: 'Dear Lord, please try to put vitamins and good things in sweets and ice-cream and not just spinach and cod-liver oil.'

A little boy, repeating the Lord's Prayer, altered it to: 'Give us this day our daily oranges'. When gently corrected and told it should be 'daily bread', he replied: 'No, I've got plenty of bread. What I want is oranges!'

We want the rules to fit our desires: the flesh commands, and God's people live under bondage, strain, defeat.

Children often have a gentle logic that helps us all to see life in a wider perspective. I like the story of the little girl who returned home after visiting her grandmother who was in hospital for a knee operation.

'How's Granny?' asked her father.

'Oh, she's fine,' the little girl replied. 'It's only her leg that's not too good.'

We are all right but for this problem, but for that habit, but for this pride, this jealousy, this heartache. But the Word says we are 'created in righteousness and true holiness' (Ephesians 4:24). There are no half-measures, He wants total victory, totally self-consecrated lives, coming God's way all the time. The popular song of the seventies went: 'I did it my way … ' That is not success but utter, abject failure!

My neighbour took his son to see a football cup-tie. Their team managed to beat their opponents from the other side of the river, much to everyone's surprise, for they'd always been unfortunate enough to lose in the past.

'That's answered my prayer, Daddy – I prayed that our team would win,' said the boy afterwards.

'Supposing that a little boy on the other side had also prayed that his team might win – what then?' asked his father.

'Oh,' the boy replied, aged six, 'in that case it would have been a draw!'

There is no draw. We always win by a big score with Jesus. He plans no defeats for us. He has no failures. We can rely on Him. He sponsors no flops!

TERRIBLE POWER

If we are One with Him, we are many times victors. What did He promise in Exodus Chapter 34? This is the chapter for the anointed ones, the surrendered ones, this is our inheritance, the promise of God's terrible power:

> The Lord descended ... and stood there ... and announced – 'I am the merciful and gracious God, slow to anger and rich in steadfast love and truth ... forgiving their sins ... This is the contract I am making with you, I will do miracles such as never have been done anywhere on the earth, and all the people shall see the power of the Lord – the terrible power, that I shall display through you ... ' (Exodus 34:6–7,10).

I had a great crusade when I was a young evangelist with Pastor George Stormont then minister of the thriving Bethshan Tabernacle in Longsight, Manchester. He had been a compatriot of Smith Wigglesworth, and I remember a story he told of that notable, anointed, mighty holy man.

When Smith Wigglesworth stayed in our home once, he came down early one morning and told me, 'God spoke to me on your bed.'

'What did he say?' I asked.

'He said, "Wigglesworth, I am going to burn you all up, until there is no more Wigglesworth, only Jesus."'

'Standing at the foot of our stairs, he raised his hands to heaven, and with tears running down his cheeks, he cried, "O, God, come and do it! I don't want them to see me any more – only Jesus!"'

'If I had to sum up the man Smith Wigglesworth as I knew him, that one statement would be it. He lived so that people would only see Jesus.'

C. S. Lewis wrote eloquently about this crucifixion of the old life:

The Christian way is different: harder, and easier. Christ says, 'Give Me All. I don't want so much of your time and so much of your money and so much of your work: I want You. I have not come to torment your natural self, but to kill it. No half-measures are any good. I don't want to cut off a branch here and a branch there – I want to have the whole tree down. I don't want to drill the tooth, or crown it, or stop it, but to have it out. Hand over the whole natural self, all the desires which you think innocent as well as the ones you think wicked – the whole outfit. I will give you a new self instead. In fact, I will give you Myself: My own will shall become yours.'

We must grasp this heart of truth, that when we are wholly His, eye, hand, heart, soul, ear, tongue, then life is borne along by the Master for us. Then there is 'no God like you in heaven or earth' (2 Chronicles 6:14). Think of it – we have His life, His blood, His nature, His promises, His name and His power!

NO OTHER STREAM

Are you at that point of utter consecration and revelation? When it came to Abraham, he saw Him as the 'God of justice' (Genesis 18:5). For Moses it was to know Him as the 'God of righteousness' (Deuteronomy 32:4). For Nehemiah, as 'The Faithful One' (Nehemiah 9:3). Even a heathen like Nebuchadnezzar confessed: 'God is just' (Daniel 4:37), while Daniel himself attested to 'God's great righteousness' (Daniel 9:4).

Give Him whole-hearted control. Let it be Jesus! Jesus! Jesus! Nothing else but Him. Everything is a piece of cake with Jesus in charge, if you will only drink of Him – make Him the beginning and the end, your goal and daily longing.

I like the incident in Chapter 2 of Lewis' *The Silver Chair*, where Jill, the Lion (the Christ) talk about the life-giving stream (His mercy, grace and Spirit):

'Are you not thirsty?' said the Lion.

'I'm *dying* of thirst,' said Jill.

'Then drink,' said the Lion.

'May I – could I – would you mind going away while I do?' said Jill.

The Lion answered this only by a look and a very low growl. And as Jill gazed at its motionless bulk, she realized that she might as well have asked the whole mountain to move aside for her convenience.

The delicious rippling noise of the stream was driving her nearly frantic.

'Will you promise not to – do anything to me, if I do come?' said Jill.

'I make no promise,' said the Lion.

Jill was so thirsty now that, without noticing it, she had come a step nearer.

'*Do* you eat girls?' she said.

'I have swallowed up girls and boys, women and men, kings and emperors, cities and realms,' said the Lion. It didn't say this as if it were boasting, nor as if it were sorry, nor as if it were angry. It just said it.

'I daren't come and drink,' said Jill.

'Then you will die of thirst,' said the Lion.

'Oh dear!' said Jill, coming another step nearer. 'I suppose I must go and look for another stream then.'

'There is no other stream,' said the Lion.

A RED-HOT CHURCH

As Laura, aged six, was having her bath, she suddenly asked:

'How does the water get in the pipes?'

Mum explained that it comes from lochs away up in the hills, through big pipes into the town.

'You remember, last Sunday when we were out in the car, we passed a loch with swans on it. That's one of them.'

Laura's face lit up. 'Next Sunday, can we go and see the HOT loch?' she asked.

People are flocking to the hot churches, to a body full of God's fire and love, a church full of vision that exalts our Lord Jesus Christ. A church that broadens its boundaries and stretches its horizons, that extends the arena of its assignments.

We are to penetrate the Kingdom of Darkness with the Kingdom of Light. For through the miracles of Christ today a flood of divine light is coming to multitudes.

A lady had been a big gambler, so that her children hardly had any food. She came to my crusade in Ripon, North Yorkshire, and was instantly saved. Three months later she told me, when I was in that area again, she never put a bet on for all that time, yet formerly she was in the bookmakers every day. She now had plenty of money for food and clothes for her kiddies. WONDERFUL, GLORIOUS JESUS!

A few years ago, I was in a Republican town near the border with Eire in County Sligo, they had buried a terrorist shot by the army three weeks before and a third of the town turned out. God healed a little child who could not walk, had never even stood before, on the first night, an immediate effect through the work of the Holy Spirit. The child stood, took a few steps, then the next night the child came, began to walk on its own. A blind lady saw and the whole town was stirred! Hundreds came to the large venue, even filling the gallery for the first time for many decades. This is the red-hot Gospel working today in the lives of the dying, despairing, sick and decadent.

In the past year I've seen drunkards made sober, alcoholics give up all drinking, gamblers stop all betting, porn readers burn their dirty books. I've also seen men and women leaving their lovers to go back to their wives and husbands again, debts being paid up, long-standing bills settled, drugs and addictions being eradicated – hundreds of lives miraculously changed and their life-styles radically altered. This is the power of the Gospel today.

John Wesley said, 'The Church has only one task that is to save souls.' Christ at the centre puts fire into our bellies and souls. His presence in the middle and in first place stirs us to action, for

He is not terrible but tender,
He is not a dictator but a deliverer,
He is not forbidding but forgiving,
He is not intractable but invincible.

ARE YOU ONE WHO IS LAYING HOLD OF HIS POWER?

9

ALL THE WAY

I was being interviewed on a well-known BBC broadcast a little while ago, when the interviewer challenged me – 'How do we know Christianity is the right religion seeing it is not the oldest religion?' Seeing Christ came two thousand years ago and there were religions prior to this, he thought he had caught me out! I also thought he had caught me out! But God flashed a scripture into my mind. How important it is to memorize scripture – what we put in comes out. Jesus said: 'In that day I will tell you what you ought to say'. How true. God reminds us, 'brings it to our remembrance', if we have worked hard to put it in.

God flashed in my mind in that BBC studio these words from John 17:5, words of Jesus to the Father: 'Glorify Thou Me *with the same glory I had with You before the foundation of the earth.*'

'According to that,' I pointed out to the sceptical 'big man' questioning me, 'the Son always had the glory with the Father, right back *before* Creation, so it must be the oldest religion. And as you have just said, if it's the oldest religion it must be the right one!'

He looked at me, astonished, then quickly replied, red-faced, 'Yes, Reverend Banks, you must be right … ' and moved on to another question.

Tens of thousands heard on that BBC programme how Christ came all the way, through the millenniums of time to visit us, to be alongside us, to favour us, to be a friend to us. In Colossians, Paul spells out his longing for all believers to go all the way with their Saviour. The Apostle longed that all through life God should be real to his people. It reads:

> For this reason ... we do not cease to pray for you and to ask, that you may be filled with the knowledge of His will in all wisdom and spiritual understanding ... that you may walk worthy of the Lord, fully pleasing Him, being fruitful in every good work and increasing in the knowledge of God, strengthened with all might, according to His glorious power, for all patience and long-suffering with joy, giving thanks to the Father who has qualified us to be partakers of the inheritance in the light. (Colossians 1:9–12)

We are made to soar above life's mundane matters. Christ is the open door out of the cage of carnalities, earthy living, low ideals, failure, worldliness and spiritual inadequacies that imprison us.

MADE TO FLY

When I visit the zoo, I skip the eagles' cage. I can't stand the pain of seeing those majestic birds sit there on their perches day after day, their burnished brown wings draped over them like an ill-fitting old coat. They were created for the heights, to dance among the clouds, not to be prisoners in a cage. Those birds were made to fly.

Many people who profess that they are Christ's

men and women are like those caged eagles. They are made to live as free citizens of heaven, but they are imprisoned by their own ways. Their condition must break God's heart. He knows what they could become, but they have put themselves in a cage. And the irony is that it is a cage with open doors.

God always gives His best to those who leave the choice with Him. 'Unless the LORD builds the house, they labour in vain who build it' (Psalm 127:1).

I vividly remember a man saying to me, 'I'll go to church and give. But I'm not going to get too involved. I'm going to concentrate on my career.' Another man admitted, 'I know I shouldn't have gotten a divorce, but I think I'm entitled to some happiness.' Both of these men were really saying, 'I don't care what God says. I'm going to do things my way.'

Solomon followed much the same path for a period in his life. After building the temple for the glory of God, he was far too lavish in erecting his palace, too preoccupied with showy horses and chariots, too status-conscious in his marriages to many pagan wives. As a result, his kingdom was marred by war and internal strife, and his home was in disarray (1 Kings 10 & 11). Some Bible scholars believe that in his later years Solomon wrote Psalm 127 out of his own bitter experience. He had discovered at last the futility of going his own way.

Our way is the path of human wisdom and self-reliance. It leads to frustration and emptiness. God's way involves trusting Him, obeying Him and depending on Him. It leads to satisfaction and joy – in part on earth but fully in heaven. Each day let's choose to live God's way.

God is looking for 100 per cent believers. I like Tozer's plea that: 'The minister himself should simply carry into the pulpit on Sunday the same spirit which has characterized him all week long. He should not need to adopt another voice nor speak in a different tone. The subject matter would necessarily differ from that of his ordinary conversation, but the mood and attitude expressed in his sermons should be identical with his daily living.'

He was telling us that God looks for you and I to go all the way, as much for ministers as for 'laity'. We are all called to 'full-time' work for the Lord. We are also called to be 'full' of the Lord, and to be 'fully' for the Lord! Paul says in Colossians: 'We have not stopped praying for you'. He asks God to 'fill' the Colossians with the knowledge of His will in 'all' spiritual wisdom and understanding. He wants them to please God in 'every' way, bearing fruit in 'every' good work, 'growing' in the knowledge of God. He prays that they may be strengthened with 'all' power, that they may have 'great' endurance and patience. It is a prayer for the very best God can give, a prayer for 100 per cent Christianity.

Without the full power of God our Christian lives are disappointing. An old American Archbishop penned the words of the rhyme:

If all the sleeping will wake up,
All the lukewarm folk will fire up,
All the crooked will straighten up,
All the depressed folk will cheer up,
All the estranged folk will make up,

All the gossip folk will shut up,
All the dry bones will shake up,
And the true believers stand up,
All the Church members show up,
To honour Him who was lifted up,
Then we can have the world's greatest Renewal.

Paul prays that the Colossians may be filled 'with the knowledge of His will through all spiritual wisdom and understanding'. When Paul speaks about God's will, he is not thinking just about the details of individual lives or even the strategy for our church life. In Ephesians 1:9–11, he speaks about 'the mystery of His will' as a plan which spans the whole of time and affects all creation, a plan which puts Christ at the centre and makes Him sovereign over everything.

How often our thinking is narrow and self-centred, like the parody of prayer: 'God bless me and my wife, our Joe and his wife, we four, no more, Amen!' God wants to stretch our vision and fire our imaginations. He wants to deliver us from our petty self-centredness and open our eyes to His great, eternal plan.

THE MAN WHO CAN

When Paul talks about 'all spiritual wisdom and understanding', he envisages not a shallow grasp of Christian truth, but layers of knowledge, wisdom and understanding.

When you learn to drive, you need knowledge. You may have read the Highway Code and a driving manual, but when you first get behind the wheel you realize that theory is not enough. You need practical experience. Proficiency doesn't come easily or quickly, but we get there with practice and patience. So, you pass your test; you know how to drive, but that is not enough. With knowledge, there has to be wisdom.

You may know how to overtake a tractor and trailer laden with hay on a narrow hill, but would it be wise? And what happens if you break down? Do you understand enough about the car to be able to put things right? And if you don't, do you know a man who can?

Knowledge, wisdom and understanding – these are essential qualities not just for driving but for living! In Colossians, Chapter Two, Paul goes on to say (of Christians he ministers to): 'My purpose is ... that they may have the full riches of complete understanding, in order that they may know the mystery of God, namely, Christ, in whom are hidden all the treasures of wisdom and knowledge' (Colossians 2:2–3).

For instruction, insight and understanding, when things go wrong, Christ is 'the man who can'.

RUN TO WIN

God wants winners, He can do only a measure of fulfilling and achievement in our lives unless we are entirely one with Him, 100 per cent with Him all the way. The old verse goes:

We must fix our eyes on Jesus
  If we're going to win the race –
Working hard at godly living,
  Trusting in His saving grace.

It's as true in life as in running: only the determined achieve their goals. Olympic medals don't go to overweight businessmen who puff around the track for exercise.

Eric Liddell, whose story is told in the film *Chariots of Fire,* illustrates this principle. Just before the first turn in a 400 metre race, Eric was shoved off balance, and he stumbled onto the infield grass. When he looked up, he saw the others pulling away. With a look of intense determination, Eric jumped to his feet, and with his back cocked and his arms flailing he rushed ahead. He was determined not only to catch up with the pack but to win. And he did!

This was the kind of fervour that the Apostle Paul brought to his ministry. In 1 Corinthians 9:24 he said, 'Do you not know that those who run in a race all run, but one receives the prize? Run in such a way that you may obtain it.' Paul saw himself as an athlete competing for a great prize, straining every muscle, nerve, and sinew to get to the finish line. And what's the prize? Not a temporary reward, but 'an imperishable crown' (1 Corinthians 9:25).

For us Christians, victory is possible. So let's run as though we want to win! Remember, WINNERS NEVER QUIT AND QUITTERS NEVER WIN.

LET'S GET GROWING

To gain the prize, eat the cake, to go through to victory after victory, to be of real precious use to God, we must grow and grow in spiritual things. 'Grow in the grace and knowledge of our Lord and Saviour Jesus Christ' (2 Peter 3:18).

Several years ago, my wife's interest in flowers had

our home resembling a nursery. There's something about the presence of growing plants that I find very enjoyable. As I daily inspected their progress, I gained from my little green friends a new appreciation of the joy and necessity of the wonderful process of growth.

As Christians, we too are like plants. We should put down our roots, break up through the earth, spread out our branches, and burst into blossom. Such a thriving condition, however, isn't always evident in our lives. It's so easy to become bored and listless in the bland routine of our daily activities. Often we just hang on and merely exist without moving steadily toward maturity and fruitfulness.

At such times we are at a spiritual standstill and must allow Jesus the 'Sun of Righteousness' (Malachi 4:2) to warm our hearts anew with His love. We must send our roots deep into the Word of God by meditating on it day and night (Psalm 1:2). Then we will be like a fruitful tree planted by rivers of living water, and our branches will extend outward in an ever-increasing influence and witness. They will be filled with blossoms that reflect the beauty of righteous living. If we've become dormant, let's get growing!

WHEN GROWTH STOPS – DECAY BEGINS

If God can make a tiny seed
Into a flower so fair,
What can He make, O soul, of thee
Through study, faith, and prayer?

Let's look at one more verse from Colossians: 'We pray this in order that you may live a life worthy of the Lord and may please Him in every way: bearing fruit in every good work, growing in the knowledge of God' (Colossians 1:10).

Knowing God's will is always practical. It means being part of God's work in the world. What makes us decide to live our lives a certain way? Here are some unspoken attitudes:

'I do what I like as long as I can get away with it.'

'I do it if there's no harm in it.'

'I do it if it's a good thing to do.'

'I do it if it's the right thing to do.'

We can probably see all these motives somewhere in our lives, but most people would agree that the second two are much better than the first two. However, none of these is a truly Christian attitude. They all come well short of 100 per cent.

Look carefully at what Paul actually says – not 'that you may live a good life' but 'that you may live a life worthy of the Lord'. The Christian's life must be consistent. The thing that made the life of Jesus so exceptional was His relationship with His Father. Jesus said: 'I always do what pleases Him' (John 8:46). Always – that's a big, big word.

The guidelines which should regulate our actions are these:

Are they consistent with the character of God revealed in Christ ('worthy of the Lord')?

Do they deepen my relationship with God because it's what pleases Him (pleasing Him 'in every way')?

Are they the product of my life in God, just as fruit is the product of the tree from which it grows ('bearing fruit in every good work')?

Do I know God well enough to be sure that my actions are what He really wants ('growing in the knowledge of God')?

Living by these standards does not come naturally; it comes supernaturally, and that is why Paul puts it into prayer.

GOD'S JEALOUS SPIRIT.

God can give such masterly victory and authority. It depends on how Jesus reigns in us, and what percentage we have given of our self to Him, and how much of Him resides in us. There's no room for double occupancy in the Christian's heart. God yearns for His control of us, and for Christ to sit upon the throne of our hearts alone.

To eat the cake, to walk free, to glide through life with enjoyment and satisfaction in our spiritual lives, and to win with ease, costs all that there is of us.

A minister tells the story:

Shep, the newest member of our family, is a young Shetland sheep-dog who openly displays his jealously when I kiss my wife. He doesn't snarl or bite, but in the language of barking he seems to be saying, 'Hey, Master, you belong to me!' His jealousy gives me a good feeling. After all, don't we all like someone to care that much about us?!

There's another kind of jealousy – a righteous jealousy – at work in the life of every Christian. It's not the yearning of a subject for his master, like that of the dog Shep, but of the Master for His subject. As James wrote, 'Do you think that the scripture says in vain, the Spirit who dwells in us yearns jealously?' (James 4:5).

When we lust, covet, and create strife, we embrace the world's values and this stirs up God's jealousy. He continually longs to keep us near to Him. He corrects, rebukes, comforts, guides, and urges us to get to know Him better. This pure possessiveness doesn't stifle or demean us, but uplifts and liberates because it is full of grace and truth. That's why He wants us all to Himself.

Thank God for His jealous Spirit.

TEST YOUR REACTIONS

By God's grace we can think spiritually and live our lives in a way that pleases God. In the last analysis, our thoughts and actions are our own: we initiate them; we control them. But what about the way other people treat us? What are our reactions?

This is the point of the Book of Job. God said: 'Look at My servant Job; look at his actions,' and Satan said, 'Fine, but let's test his reactions.' The rest of the book is about the results of that challenge, Satan bombarded Job with every dark weapon in his unholy capability.

As Paul prayed, he asked God that the Colossian believers would have truly Christian reactions, and he named four.

First, *endurance*. This applies to difficult circumstances, when things go terribly wrong and disaster strikes. Endurance is the ability to survive under pressure.

The second reaction is *patience*. This is the ability to cope with difficult people. 'To dwell above with saints we love – oh that will be glory! To dwell below with saints we know – well that's a different story!'

Awkward people, whinging people, depressed people, demanding people – how do we react? Paul says, 'I'm praying for patience.'

That would be remarkable enough, but Paul has not finished yet. He goes on to say ' ... and joyfully giving thanks'. But it could also be linked with what goes before – not just endurance and patience, not just 'great' endurance and patience, but great endurance and patience 'with *joy*'!

And on top of that, genuine *thankfulness* to God. Not giving thanks for the bad things, but in spite of them.

Reactions like that do not emerge from the resources of the human spirit; they have come to us from God, and that is why Paul prays for them. It is only as we are 'Strengthened with all power according to His glorious might', that such a quality of living will be seen – mature living, 100 per cent Christianity.

Giving every ounce of ourselves, so we go all the way, we gain the cake, we win the prize, we reach God's goals for us smoothly and with ease.

10

YOUR ANOINTING, YOUR HOPE

If you despise what you have and are, and where you find you are placed by God, your spiritual life will drain away. That is where the presence of God is, in your obedience to your call, your acceptance of your task or job for the Lord God.

Bezaleel in Exodus 31:2 was filled with the Spirit, with knowledge and wisdom for the work of the Tabernacle. He was anointed and found God's presence and blessing as he stayed in his vocation. God anoints all His children, all His servants for whatever He sets them out to do.

Don't walk out of your vocation. God is present with you there. Miriam walked out of her anointing and lost the presence of God. The anointing can lift when you start doing something other than what God has given you to do. You lose the blessings, and lose His personal presence when you start going your own ways and walking in disobedience. Miriam was struck down with leprosy, and although she later repented, was sent outside the camp into the wilderness for seven days, then God healed her. But what dishonour, all because she did not stay where her Saviour was.

Uzziah, in 2 Chronicles 26:16, after a brilliant and successful God-blessed reign, goes and seeks to be a priest and burns incense on the holy altar. Instead of staying in touch with the presence of the Lord, he goes off out of his ministry and breaks an oath with the Lord. With His presence we can do anything. If God shows up, we are mighty winners; if we lose that, we are paupers.

DON'T RUN AWAY FROM THE CALL

Many preachers either speak on history – what happened yesterday, or prophesy – what is going to happen tomorrow ... but I'm interested only in the now. We can live on an experience, a blessing, some spiritual feast we had 20 years ago. God wants us to live in 'the now experience'. Winston Mews, the great Canadian Gospel preacher, used to say, 'If you stop getting new revelation, fresh touches, you will die spiritually.'

I need a mountain-top experience regularly to stay alive. In Great Yarmouth our workers and local Christians put out 40,000 invitations to my great 'Miracle Explosion' Crusade there. The whole city was shaken, everyone heard about the meetings and the miracles of God. They said, as in Matthew: 'Never has it been seen like this in the land before.'

But it costs much, in seeking God. When I went to the next town the following day, a small country town in Suffolk, the queues to get in wound up the street. The sick were coming in hundreds. But as I arrive with my staff at this new town, I see fresh challenges. God gives me masses to minister to. I cannot say: 'I want to rest. I'm too tired. Come back tomorrow night.' The BBC is there. The newspapers are there. Often, TV is present, breathing down my neck, the pressure to produce is great. I must have His presence! I must have His up-to-the-moment anointing. I must hear His voice again today for these starving, sad, dying, grieving people.

Pastors ring daily: 'Can you come to our city?' 'What about our town?' or, 'You have never been in this state or county.' Demands, pressures, requests, desperation. One call after another. Be faithful where you are. Don't come out of your calling. Don't despise your anointing and place. Don't run away from the call.

The whole world runs to the feet of the man who stays in the presence of God. Your job may be small, insignificant, tiny or second-rate. Do it well, and God will promote you. Benny Hinn used to give out the music to the choir for Kathryn Kuhlman's meetings. Recently some of his rallies were topping 28,000 to 30,000 in a service. He started a choir, and the Kathryn Kuhlman foundation donated all the music from her old office to him. What a lesson to learn. One young lad doing his job well, giving out music to the singers, now gets all the great lady's music personally for his own 2,000 member choirs, for the rallies where he preaches to multitudes! REAP AND YOU SOW!

I spent four years training under Herbert Harrison, one of Britain's most successful pastors. He saw a small work begin with 20 people and grow to 600 or more, and, literally 10,000 in real numbers were made disciples and added to Christ's Church. I was a right hand to him, but it was impossible to get close to him. I must have added something like 200 good, firm, disciples to his church through personal soul-winning, running small missions, and doing bus evangelism in those years. Yet I think I preached for him only three times, and that only in smaller meetings. He never once allowed me to preach on a

Sunday night in his great Gospel meeting, although half his congregation sometimes I had brought in personally, mostly by using hired buses. But I took it on the chin. But I had to laugh recently, when it was pointed out to me that I was now preaching to the largest Sunday night Gospel meetings in the UK!

VANITY FAIR

Do your little job well. God will promote you. Don't complain, love it, do it for Jesus, keep a single eye on His glory. For many, it's quick promotion, the top tables, the big ministries and jobs. Self-centredness is the curse of the Church. We live in Vanity Fair – a quick fix – the spirit of the age is even invading the ministry.

Dean Inge said: 'He who marries the spirit of the age will find himself a widower in the next.' O.S. Guinness pointed out that today, 'Shapeliness is now next to godliness'. Reject these views. Seek and aspire to the things of the Kingdom of God. Be faithful in small things. I remember the first month I was with Herbert Harrison in Bethshan, Newcastle. 'Herbie' gave me the job nobody wanted and many others had failed in – to run a Sunday School in the roughest area of the city. Soon 200 screaming, wild, tough, undisciplined kids were shouting their heads off in my meetings. I persevered. I was spat at by this mob, but God gave me grace to tame some of them. God moved on many of them. Some got saved and stayed with us, in that church in the Newcastle ghetto.

From being spat at by an angry, whining mob to preaching the Gospel to 18,000 recently, in the Crystal Palace football ground … that's God's faithfulness!

Keep your motives clean and seek the glory of God. Be filled with compassion. Run out with the Good News. Don't look at what others are doing. Do your task well and God will see to all else. The presence of Christ is found in your walking in your calling.

Gideon, a small, weak man, tears down the altars of his father's idols when he finds his call and anointing ... BUT SADLY, later, loses it by making an ephod image, causing the whole land to sin.

Moses, the meekest man on earth, leads forth a whole nation under God's guidance as he walks in his calling ... BUT SADLY, angers God by smiting the rock.

Solomon builds the magnificent temple ... BUT SADLY is led astray by many lovers.

Hezekiah gets fifteen years extra life from God, changing the mind of the Almighty! ... BUT SADLY squanders it away by helping his enemies!

Demas, was a member of the historic Apostolic team that shook the face of the earth ... BUT SADLY turned away to go back to this present worldly society!

Don't cut Him off! Stay in your call. Don't walk away from the anointing. Don't despise what you have. Don't leave His presence. Not self, but Christ all the way. I'm not interested in anything that has not got Jesus in the centre of it. Look always only to Jesus. Take the presence of Jesus out and we have only noise in a service. BUT AS YOU DIE, HE LIVES.

HUMILITY

Hudson Taylor, a dedicated missionary, the first to China, wrote: 'If I have a fortune, China should have it. If I had a thousand lives, China would have them. No! Not China, but Christ! Can we do too much for Him?' Give yourself away. Stay in your task, your job, your place, your call. When I've communed with Him, been in His presence, I can go into one of my miracle services unbeatable. God says, 'Trust Me. Stay where you are, where I've put you. For come hell or high water, not one hair on your head will be lost to the enemy.'

We need some believers who can sleep in the boat when the storm reaches its peak, like Jesus did on the sea of Galilee. Panic reigns today. Pandemonium holds sway. Hopelessness prevails. But in the midst of it all, we must not lose our nerve. Staying in our high calling keeps the presence of God.

Jesus said, 'Humble yourselves'. Solomon wrote, 'To the humble God shows favour' (Proverbs 3:34). Winston Churchill said: 'One thing man has been unable to conquer, is himself.' Martin Luther, when asked what were the three greatest virtues in the Christian faith, replied: 'Humility, Humility, Humility.' Believers are affected by the greediness, the pampered self-life, the touchiness, and self-infatuation of our age. Self-crucifixion is the way to submission. In that we are able to stay in our call and thus know His presence mightily. 'The Lord takes pleasure in His people. He adorns the humble with victory' (Psalm 149:4).

Humility is a release from hiding and pretending to be something we are not. It is a longing in our heart for communion with God. Cry out with the Psalmist, 'My heart thirsts for God, the living God' (Psalm 42:2 NIV).

The apostle Paul lived in a cruel and pessimistic world. When he wrote his letter to the Romans, the destruction of Jerusalem was just around the corner, and the great empire of Rome already showed the cracks which would lead to its downfall a few centuries later. Yet Paul could speak about 'the God of hope', the God who inspires hope, the God who is the ground of hope.'For no matter how many promises God has made they are "Yes" in Christ' (2 Corinthians 1:20). However long the night, however dark the skies, God gives hope to those who look at His promises. The God of hope will never break His word.

Hope in the Bible is a very different thing from what passes for hope among those who lack faith. In Dickens' *David Copperfield*, Mr Micawber was always 'Waiting for something to turn up'. Such optimism in the face of life's disappointments is often trusting more to luck than judgement.

Like the two tramps in *Waiting for Godot*, many people wait for good fortune, or a better world. But Godot never came. Samuel Becket's hard message is that he never will. Things won't get better, and life is ultimately absurd and meaningless.

In contrast, Paul says that God gives joy and peace in believing. Joy and peace are linked here with faith. He doubtless remembered the words of the Lord Jesus, 'My peace I give to you ... that your joy may be complete' (John 14:27; John 15:11). Often those whose lives radiate peace and serenity are those who have lived through incredible suffering and trials. The greater the breaking, crushing, shaking, squeezing, dying to self, often through great trial, the stronger the hope, it seems. Paul himself, who experienced such 'in season and out of season', such 'abasement', and was 'pressed down but not destroyed' as he put it, could yet recommend: 'Experience hope' (Rom 5:4), that 'We might through patience have hope', and 'abound in hope" (Romans 15:13). 'Now abideth faith, hope, love' (1 Corinthians 13:13). Hope is tied to faith strongly. John Bunyan wrote: 'Hope is never ill when faith is well.'

The storms of life increase or wipe out hope. Somebody said: 'Remember the darkest hour only lasts 60 minutes!' God is in there for every second with you, increasing your hope, if faith is real and strong.

I like Neumark, the German theologian's verse, written 350 years ago, but is as true today.

If thou but suffer God to guide thee,
    And hope in Him through
all thy ways,
    He'll give thee strength
whate'er betide thee,
    And bear thee through the evil days;
Who trust in God's unchanging love
    Builds on the rock that
nought can move.

THE GOD OF HOPE NEVER BREAKS HIS WORD

Life has often been hard for Beryl and John who live in Cleveland. But the lowest point came recently. Beryl gave up nursing some time back due to ill health and John was made redundant two years ago.

They're on income support and their rent is paid, for which they're grateful, but John can't help feeling humiliated. 'I don't have the dignity of paying my own rent,' he'd say.

One Saturday they had so many bills to pay they couldn't settle them all, and then they couldn't buy anything for Sunday dinner. They were so depressed that they talked long and seriously about ending it all – but eventually they decided that they couldn't go through with it.

That night in bed John, who had a cold, began to snore. Beryl, unable to sleep, slipped through to the spare room. At 6 a.m. the door burst open, and she heard John gasp with relief. When he'd woken and found Beryl gone, he'd jumped to the conclusion that she had gone ahead and taken her life.

That morning, before John went to work in the garden of an elderly woman in the village, he hugged Beryl, and kissed her tenderly. As time went on and he didn't return, it was Beryl's turn to feel anxious and fearful, wondering if his loving embrace had meant he wouldn't be coming home – ever.

Of course, he did – and they fell into each other's arms. Amid tears, they decided no matter how hard times were, they were richer than most because they had each other – although it took a snore and a cuddle to prove it to them. Somehow the egg and chips they had for dinner that night was the best meal they'd ever shared!

Through thankfulness hope was restored. Many have become unthankful and lost their note of praise. They have looked at the outward circumstances, gone down into oblivion and hopelessness. God wants to lift us in the storms.

Irina Ratushinskaya, after years under the grey skies of a Soviet labour camp, could write an autobiography entitled, *Grey is the Colour of Hope*. Only those whose life is built firmly on the rock of faith can experience joy and peace in believing – especially when the skies are black, and the storms of adversity lash our frail humanity.

The great biblical example is Abraham. When all hope, from a human point of view, was impossible, he hoped on, trusting in God's promise (see Romans 4:18–21). John Calvin related faith and hope like this: 'The word "hope" I take for faith; and indeed hope is nothing else but the constancy of faith.'

Paul prays that the God of hope will fill us, 'so that [we] will overflow with hope by the power of the Holy Spirit'. Hope is not something we can keep to ourselves. It is contagious. Paul in the ship, telling his companions to take courage when shipwreck was a certainty, is an example of overflowing hope. His faith in God's promise enabled him to give hope to others.

Only those whose life is built firmly on the rock of faith can experience hope. 'According to my earnest expectation and hope, ... that I shall continue with the joy of faith ... that your rejoicing may be more abundant' (Philippians 1:20,25–26). The blessing to others, the rejoicing to the downcast, the discouraged, and the lost, or a church with weakness of faith is outstanding when we ourselves have a burning hope. God said in Zechariah 9:11: 'As for you also, because of the blood of your covenant, I will set your prisoners free from the waterless pit.'

Because Jesus paid the price through His sacrificial atonement, we sought faith. We go through the bruising, the dying, the cringing, and the brokenness with Him. Faith shines through; we become strong in the Holy Spirit and the anointing. We become one, in the 'fellowship of His sufferings', with Jesus. And as a result, faith keeps us steady in the storm, empowering our hope, increasing our anointing.

11

REAL SUCCESS

A well-known, elderly Hollywood actress said that life is such a mixture of good and bad that she looks forward to oblivion when she dies. She has lots of money and is famous, but is she really a success?

By contrast, Basil Oliver enjoyed neither money nor fame during the last 30 years of his life. He lived in the London YMCA and worked as an office boy, running errands and serving food, mailing letters for people and making himself useful. He was always smiling, and when he died peacefully in his room at 85 years of age, his death went unnoticed by the world. But the great Bible commentator William Barclay wrote of this man: 'I'm sure that His Master Jesus Christ knew him very well, I will miss him, but I'm sure God will be glad to have him.' Basil was a success!

Psalm 84 was also written by a successful man:

Happy are those who are strong in the Lord, who want above all else to follow Your foot-steps. When they walk through the valley of weeping, it ... will become a pool of blessing ... They will grow constantly in strength ... I would rather be a doorman in the temple of my God than live in palaces of worldly wickedness ... No good thing will God withhold from those who walk along His paths (Psalm 84:5–6, 10–11, Living Bible).

It's better to be faithful than famous. Jeremiah wrote: 'And do you seek great things for yourself? Do not seek them' (Jeremiah 45:5). English pastor and author F. B. Meyer said: 'Don't waste your time waiting for and longing for large opportunities which may never come, but faithfully handle the little things that are always claiming your attention.' I like Bernheivels words:

> Teach me to do the humble task
> The very best I can,
> And not to look for greater calls
> That may oppose Thy plan.

An elderly widow, restricted by her activities, was eager to serve Christ. After praying about this, she realized that she could bring blessing to others by playing the piano. The next day she placed this small advert in the paper: 'PIANIST WILL PLAY HYMNS BY PHONE DAILY FOR THOSE WHO ARE SICK OR DESPONDENT – THE SERVICE IS FREE.'

The notice included the number to dial. When people called, she would ask, 'What hymn would you like?' Within a month, her playing had brought cheer to several hundred people. Many of them freely poured out their hearts and troubles to her, and she was able to bless, help and encourage countless numbers. Today the Saviour asks you: 'What is that in your hand?' as He asked Moses. Are you willing to use what He has given you for His glory? The verse goes:

Use now the 'rod' that's in your hand,
  Count not your talent small;
God does not ask of you great things,
  Just faithfulness – that's all!

God often uses small matches to light great torches!
Are you putting energy, time, money, talents, and
your health to good effect? Remember tying up your
first shoe laces? My mum did them for me (she spoilt
me, of course) till I was nearly seven years old. Of
course, there were no 'slip-ons' in those ancient
times!

Those shoes that fasten with velcro are grand for
little fingers which haven't yet mastered the art of
tying shoe laces. Though not yet five, Craig is at
school. But when he came home the other afternoon,
he was limping. 'My shoes hurt,' he complained to
his mother.

When Mum looked closer, she saw why. 'Of course
your feet hurt, silly – you've got them on the wrong
feet!'

Craig stopped his sobs and gave his mother an
indignant look. 'Mummy,' he said, 'these are the only
feet I've got!'

We must give God what we have, it may be the
only virtue, talent, or possibility.

Small people are the most important. Watching the
rapt attention of a group of children from a children's home recently, I was touched in my heart as I
saw them, overjoyed with Disney's film *Aladdin*. My
other favourite Disney film is *Bambi*. I recalled after
seeing the response of the little ones that day, the
story of the deer in that film, which for 50 years had
brought such happiness to millions. Yet few know

the name of the major illustrator who so vividly brought to life the animals in the forest in such a marvellous, delightful way.

His name was Jake Day. When he died at 90, no mention appeared in the newspapers. A man whose work meant so much to so many, yet whose name meant nothing to those outside his own circle.

We take for granted that there will be milk on the doorstep each morning, but we don't know who milks the cows. We look forward to mail popping through the letter box, but have no idea who sorts it. We are all dependent on someone we may not know. And while we may not all be as talented as Jake Day, the world turns because the small – not the great – use what they have!

Great things are little things done with a desire to please God. As the poet put it:

> *Show me the fullness of the joy*
> *Which comes from serving Thee;*
> *Let me not seek the pomp and praise*
> *Which men may offer me.*

WHO IS THE GREATEST?

I was standing in former East Germany, next to where the old Iron Curtain fell. I was on a four week preaching tour in Luxembourg and Austria and on into Germany. It had been hectic with crowded services with new Churches springing up. After I had taken my photographs – a rare opportunity – for although I've preached in 34 nations of the world, I've had few opportunities to see much of it, only through a plane window, from a car or train. So many engagements are booked, so many pastors want to talk to me, and so many crowds waiting to receive the Word of the Lord.

Many of the homes in East of Germany that I saw, and was told, as we drove through the villages, had not been painted outside (except the Communist officials' homes) for 45 years! Roads were a ruin, but the new united Germany was building new ones as fast as chickens lay eggs. Don't those Germans work! I saw houses being painted and electric power lines being put underground. They had been strung from poles for five decades, leaving people often without light or heat in times of winds and storms. Now roads were springing up everywhere. All the people seemed to be painting, building, repairing, trying to catch up. It was a hive of activity, ingenuity and expansion.

The East Germans had blared across the heavily-fortified Iron Curtain fencing with loudspeakers, each day for five decades, dropping literature in the West. Their slogan: 'WE ARE THE GREATEST!'. Yet they shot hundreds trying to get away from the Communist paradise! I stood where so many had been killed or wounded, then devoured by hungry Dobermann guard dogs. What inhumanity and evil! Communism had set up not a 'heaven' or the 'greatest' society, but a 'hell on earth'.

Who is the greatest? Even Jesus was asked that question. But if the truth were told, we are all good at the who-is-the-greatest syndrome. The 'biggest', the 'most penetrating', the 'best-produced', 'the most significant'; read the blurbs on the record sleeves, book covers, leaflets for seminars, conferences, businesses, conventions. The whole thing is as old as the disciples' questions on who would be the greatest, or who should sit on Jesus' right hand or left in the coming kingdom.

It's been my privilege to preach with the greatest preachers of this generation. Ray McCauley, Leighton Ford, Dr Fred Roberts (of Durban, SA), Colin Urqhart. I've personally met and talked privately to Billy Graham, David Wilkerson, Reinhardt Bonnke, Dr Eric Hutchings, Dr Paul Yonggi Cho, Morris Cerrulo, and many others. I have had the great honour of preaching in my crusades to as many as 18,000. Yet never was I moved more than that day I stood in the basement of an Elim Christian Centre in Aberdeen.

The church building is a former theatre, the cellars were used as air raid shelters during the war. As the place is on a road, close to the docks, it was handy when the bombers came, for workmen to run to and take shelter.

The Christians had turned the cellars into a home for the beggars and homeless. That night the bell went, and one by one young and old, most in rough, poor clothing came into the cellars. There were 17 there as I stood amongst them at midnight, hot soup and a meal was enjoyed away from the cold of the September night outside. A video was playing on a small TV screen, there was light music and a warm fire. There was clothing for them, a hot shower, a friendly welcome, love, kindness, and a Christian hand of care with a prayer. Tears filled my eyes, my heart was deeply moved. I felt the presence of Christ in that place as much as amongst the greatest preachers of our age. They were the greatest. David and his helpers who did that work every day and night of the year. Two thousand homeless people had passed through the doors in the first year it was open. So impressed were the tough policemen on the beat in that dockland district that they had taken collections around the local city police stations, and given hundreds of pounds towards running the rescue home. Those Christians are the salt of the earth.

Jesus said the greatest of the kingdom was the one who was the servant of all. In His view, being a servant is not a greater thing in His kingdom – it is the greatest.

FIRST GAZE

Have you ever imagined what Bartimaeus thought of Christ before he got his sight? The crowd had told him that Jesus of Nazareth was passing by. 'Jesus, Son of David, have mercy on me!' he cried, recognizing the Lord as more than a mere man. The crowd tried to silence the blind man but he cried out all the more. 'So,' says the Bible, 'Jesus stood still.'

Think of it. The one who rules the universe stood still and gave the man his sight back! Try to imagine Bartimaeus' first gaze upon God incarnate. What do you think he imagined he would see? What would you have imagined, putting the scene in a modern setting?

A gold chain, surely! A touch of ermine, at least? Even a small gold crown? An entourage that would at least fill a suite or two at Claridges? A few public relations 'advance men'? Not a bit of it. He saw before him a weary, travel-stained man, born of a peasant woman, unheard of except in Nazareth, that most despised of all Israelite towns. Here was the One whose Word created the Grand Canyon, the rose and the constellation Orion. Who created my lovely countryside, the Cotswolds, the heart of England. 'A man of sorrows and acquainted with grief. And we hid as it were, our faces from him.' But not Bartimaeus. He gazed upon that lovely man of Galilee and immediately gave up begging. He stopped saying 'Give me, give me!' He followed Jesus in the way of servanthood.

Bartimaeus started living for Christ. He stopped living as if everyone else owed him a living and started living for Christ and others. That is the true path to greatness.

David Stanley, Elvis Presley's step-brother and personal bodyguard, speaks of his brother Rick who had said to Elvis the night before he died how a friend kept telling him how he needed to start living for Jesus. Elvis told him, 'It was high time we all started living for Jesus.' How about us? God's perfect servant is 'the King' in the kingdom – and those who serve Him know true greatness.

SUCCESSFUL FAILURES

'If anyone sins, we have an Advocate with the Father, Jesus Christ the righteous' (1 John 2:1).

The great inventor Charles Kettering suggested that we must learn to fail intelligently. He said: 'Once you've failed, analyse the problem and find out why, because each failure is one more step leading up to the cathedral of success. The only time you don't want to fail is the last time you try.'

Kettering gave these suggestions for turning failure into success:

Honestly face defeat; never fake success.
Exploit the failure; don't waste it. Learn all you can from it.
Never use failure as an excuse for not trying again.

The inventor's practical wisdom holds double meaning for the Christian. Because the Holy Spirit is constantly working in us to accomplish His good purposes (Philippians 2:13), we know that failure is never final. We cannot reclaim lost time; nor can we always make things right, although we should try. Some of the consequences of our sins can never be reversed. But we can make a new start because we have an Advocate before God – Jesus, whose death fully paid for all our sins even before we were born.

Fasick wrote:

*Failure is failing to trust and believe
That God can accomplish His purpose through you;
Failure is failing to keep on trying
To do all the Saviour has asked you to do.*

Success is failure turned inside out. I love the verse:

*If I can live a life that tells on other lives,
And make the world less full of anguish and of pain;
A life, that like the pebbles dropped upon the sea,
Sends its wide circles to a hundred shores.*

May such a life be mine, for that is God's success.

I was impressed by a church I visited, where everyone pitched in and worked and did something, not only a godly atmosphere and great praise and worship, but care and concern for others reigned.

On the Sunday I spoke, three services were scheduled: morning, afternoon, and evening. The women of the church had provided a bountiful meal to be served between the meetings for visitors who had travelled a long distance to attend.

Following the dinner, after most of the people had left, I noticed a distinguished-looking couple clearing the tables and dumping the dirty paper plates into large plastic bags. When I complimented them on what they were doing, they said matter-of-factly, 'Oh, we're the "dustbin detail". We volunteered to clean up after every church function. We consider it a ministry.' I thought, how wonderful! This man and woman were not only available to serve the Lord, but they humbly did what others might consider demeaning work. Some individuals volunteer for the more prominent and appealing forms of ministry in the church, but these dear people were glad to be what they cheerfully called 'the dustbin detail'!

The glory of life is to love, not to be loved; to give, not to get; to serve, not to be served. 'And whatever you do, do it heartily, as to the Lord and not to men' (Colossians 3:23). The Father will not forget to reward each of His children for what has been done in His Name. No act of love, no reverence of heart, no meditation on His Word will escape His memory. Have you been faithful to the Lord, only to have no one notice? Take heart! God sees your devotion. He has recorded it, and He will reward you for it. What an encouragement!

The hymn runs:

> *God takes notice of your service*
> *Freely rendered in His name;*
> *Even though by friends forgotten,*
> *You He'll honour just the same.*

Advice columnist Abigail van Buren illustrated man's ability to overcome obstacles when she wrote:

> Cripple him, and you have a Sir Walter Scott. Lock him in a prison cell, and you have a John Bunyan. Bury him in the snows of Valley Forge, and you have a George Washington. Afflict him with asthma as a child, and you have a Theodore Roosevelt. Make him play second fiddle in an obscure South American orchestra, and you have a Toscanini. Deny her the ability to see, hear, and speak, and you have a Helen Keller.

I am sure you get the point. No one has to be a loser. Take the advice:

> *Be not afraid to fail, my friend;*
> *Mistakes you're bound to make;*
> *With courage venture bravely on*
> *And try for Jesus' sake.*

12

THE SIMPLE SECRET OF
AN UNSINKABLE LIFE

Two boats passed each other on the Mississippi river one day. Two black workmen were chatting together as they toiled. One pointed over at the other passing ship. Very excited, he cried out, 'Look, there's the Captain!' Again he shouted, 'Hello Captain! Hello! Hi Captain!'

The Captain waved back vigorously, smiling broadly. The workman's joy was unstoppable. 'That's the Captain, that's the one,' he merrily shared with his mate.

The other finally got some words in. 'What's special about that governor? There are hundreds of boats on this river and a thousand captains. What's great about him?'

Most indignant, the fellow replied, 'Years ago, as a boy I fell overboard. The Captain leapt over the side into these dangerous waters and rescued me. Since then I just loves to point the Captain out!'

Do you love to point out the Captain of your Salvation? The hallmark of the unsinkable life is that type of spirit – we love our great Captain. We used to sing a song when I was a boy in the Salvation Army meetings I went to. With what gusto, and with what clapping and joy we sang it:

> I've found a friend, O such a friend,
> He loved me 'ere I knew him,

He drew me with the cords of love,
  And thus He bound me to Him.

We are encouraged by Scripture to: 'stand before the presence of the Lord' and 'sing out of the presence of the Lord', and to 'hide in the secret of Thy presence' (2 Chronicles 20:9; 2 Chronicles 16:33; Psalm 31:20). But what is the secret to this presence?

THE SECRET IS SCRIPTURE

God has re-taught me after 40 years in the ministry that there is only a continual deep sense of His enthronement and presence in one's life if Scripture fills one's mind.

Scripture is an antiseptic towards the world's filth, its carnal and godless contamination. It's like Andrews Liver Salts for the inner physical being: it refreshes, cleanses, rejuvenates. The label on that commodity reads: 'TAKE FIRST THING EVERY MORNING BEFORE BREAKFAST AND LAST THING AT NIGHT.' Good advice for the inner spiritual being also. The Word day and night, night and day and in between!

My wife purchased the whole Bible on tape some two years ago and plays it to me on aeroplanes, in the car, on trains, in the motel, caravan – first thing in the morning, at mealtimes and at night. I know a young preacher who even keeps the tapes going all night as he sleeps, so the Word is being read, filling his room, even when he is in the land of Nod! That is enthusiasm. The Word of God all night!

In Psalm 119:11 we read: 'Your word have I hidden in my heart, that I might not sin against you.'

One day a young Christian came into a mission station in Korea to visit the man who had been instrumental in his conversion to Christ. After the customary greetings, the missionary asked the reason for his coming. 'I have been memorizing some verses in the Bible,' he said, 'and I want to quote them to you.' He had walked hundreds of miles just to recite some Scripture verses to his father in the faith.

The missionary listened as he recited without error the entire Sermon on the Mount. He commended the young man for his remarkable feat of memory, then cautioned that he must not only 'say' the Scriptures but also practise them. With glowing face, the man responded, 'Oh, that is the way I learned them. I tried to memorize them but they wouldn't stick, so I hit on this plan. First, I would learn a verse. Then I would practise what the verse said on a neighbour who was not a Christian. After that, I found I could remember it.'

God said, 'Have I not spoken it, shall I not fulfil it?' To get a hold of Scripture, let Scripture get a hold of you. I like the old verse:

We learn the blessed Word of God
　To fix it firmly in our heart;
And when we act upon that Word
　Its truth from us will not depart.

True faith obeys without doubt or delay. Sper wrote:

God's Word reveals what we should know
　To live for Him each day:
His principles we must commit
　To study and obey.

Are you often side-tracked? I've got to admit it's one of my failings. The other evening, for example, I planned to phone a friend. Before I picked up the receiver I felt a draught, and found the back door was open. As I closed it, I caught sight of my cold frame and that set me wondering if the cuttings I'd put there needed watering. I brought the watering can from the shed and, after filling it, saw the kitchen tap was still dripping. I turned off the water, took a wrench from the garage, replaced the washer – and cut my finger in the process.

There were sticking plasters in the first-aid box in the car, I remembered. But while putting one on my finger, I noticed the car's rear tyre was flat. So out came the jack, off came the wheel, and on went the spare. Finally I went to water the cuttings. As I came back in, my wife, intent on her reading, raised an eyebrow. 'That was a marathon phone call,' she said. I thought it better not to go into explanations ...

'The upright shall dwell in His presence', the Psalmist claimed. Who are these rare species today? Are they not those who meditate in the Word day and night, as Psalm 1 tells us, setting the pace for the whole of that magnificent book on knowing the enthroned, living God close to us. Knowing the Bible is vital to knowing the God of the Bible. An unread Bible usually belongs to an unfed believer. We can only know His thoughts, His ways, His mind, His Will, His peace, His comforts, His powers, if we know His Word. The verse goes:

My Bible to me is a treasure house
  Where I never fail to find
The things I need from day to day
  For my heart and soul and mind.

God's living Word is the only hope for a dying world. But it must conquer us first. It must live in our hearts and minds first.

FOOD FOR OUR SOULS

Two little boys, both preachers' sons about five years of age, were sitting on the front row of the service having a really good argument. One claimed, 'My dad's the best preacher! He can preach without notes!' The other retorted, 'He's not. My dad's better than that, he can preach without thinking!'

God wants His Words, His mind, Divine thinking to fill your heart and mind and being. 'Your words were found, and I ate them, and Your Word was to me the joy ... of my heart' (Jeremiah 15:16). The Word of God is food for our souls. It fully satisfies our spiritual hunger. As we meditate upon it, our craving for spiritual knowledge, wisdom, and guidance is fulfilled.

James M. Gray, a former president of the Moody Bible Institute, commented on Jeremiah 15:16 by saying: 'There is a great difference between finding the Word and eating it ... Putting the Word into your mind is like holding food in your mouth; it allows you to get the first full taste of it ... Turning a Scripture around and around, thinking of it from many points of view, asking questions about it, and searching for its meaning in a commentary, is like chewing. It makes good assimilation possible.' Gray continued, 'The only way to hold the Word in your mind is to memorize it!'

Reading the Bible without reflecting is like eating without chewing!

Great men in the Bible meditated. Psalm 1 tells us: 'They delight in doing everything God wants them to, and day and night are always meditating on His laws, and thinking about ways to follow Him more closely' (Psalm 1:2, Living Bible). Isaac 'went out to meditate' (Genesis 24:63). Joshua was commanded, 'Thou shalt meditate therein day and night' (Joshua 1:8). David wrote, 'I will meditate on all Thy works' (Psalm 77:12). Paul said, 'meditate on these things' (1 Timothy 4:15).

Jesus said, 'If my words abide in you ... ye shall ask whatever you want and it will be given to you'. For them to abide in us, we must eat them, take them in, meditate on them.

Meditate, not just read. I read or listen to about 25 chapters a day. To meditate is to chew over, absorb in the mind, muse on, or to mutter over, or to roll over and over, to think much on ... to remember if you can.

MEDITATION

My mum used to roll the pastry on the table, flattening it with a rolling pin to smooth it. She was still making cakes, and especially scones, till the day before she died. She left me a plate of them, all fresh and ready-made! Smooth – to meditate is to smoothen the truth, to roll it over until it is clear and plain.

A church I have visited many times in Austria is run by the godly Dr Inglebert at Satteins, Western

Tyrol. Growing so much in one of the world's toughest nations, in tiny villages hardened by hundreds of years of traditions, with no Gospel witness in history, not even touched once during the Reformation. I was speaking to the crowded church recently, and took a jog up into the beautiful mountains. It was a cold January day, but the sun was shining. The white, crisp snow lay farther up the steep inclines, but I stood by a stream. The water was clean, crystal clear and sparkling, and one could have drank and washed in it. I put my hand into the cold rushing torrent and picked up a smooth stone. It had been there for hundreds of years. Once it had been rough, cutting, sharp and brittle. But now it was smooth, clean, polished almost, by millions of tons of water pouring on it. Year after year, rolling down, down. Pressure. Rushing water had smoothed it over the years. How lovely is the water of the Word, day and night, constantly flowing through us.

There are nine main ways to get to know His Word:

Read it yourself daily.
Listen to it on tape, radio or TV.
Write it out in note books.
Study it yourself, or do a course at the Church or a respected Bible School, or do a course by correspondence.
Hear it preached from sound pulpits.
Sing it often.
Memorize it.
Speak it out, the Word on your lips. A daily confession, a whole chapter a day.
And the most neglected – meditating on it, rolling it over and over until you are cleansed

and polished. Until all carnalities, unholiness, impurities are rubbed off. You are made smooth, shining through the Word.

When Joshua took over the leadership of the Israelites from Moses, an awesome task, God gave him a recipe for success: 'Do not let this Book of the Law depart from your mouth; meditate on it day and night' (Joshua 1:8). Paul encouraged the Philippians to meditate, and he exhorted the young Timothy to do the same.

There has been much talk for many years on 'Transcendental Meditation'. Hindu in origin, and humanistic in philosophy, but we are not talking about that. The main purpose of Biblical meditation is to get to know God, and His beloved son Jesus.

In Psalm 1, the one who meditates is promised 'blessedness', which means happiness and fruitfulness. He will 'not wither', never get dried up in the Christian walk, and 'whatever he does prospers'. What promises! And God never exaggerates. 'He shall be like a tree planted by streams of water, which yields its fruit in season and whose leaf does not wither. Whatever he does, prospers.'

Whenever you come to a promise in God's Word, you should look for two things. First: what God says He will do, and second what God tells us to do. If we do what He tells us, He will always fulfil His promises. The first condition is separation from sin, and separation to God. 'Blessed is the man who does not walk in the counsel of the wicked or stand in the way of sinners or sit in the seat of mockers.' The second condition is to 'delight' in His Word, that is, to take pleasure in it; and the third to 'meditate day and night'.

Meditation is certainly not letting our minds go blank. There are too many things looking for blank minds! Meditation is pondering, considering a verse of Scripture, word by word, in complete dependence on the Holy Spirit to illumine that Word to you.

Three things are essential for the real absorption of truth: knowledge, understanding and wisdom. Knowledge is having the facts. Understanding is knowing what the facts are about. Wisdom is the ability to apply to our lives and circumstances what we know and understand. There is no use in knowledge without understanding. David said: 'I have more insight than all my teachers, for I meditate' (Psalm 119:99).

Meditation gives us understanding. Meditation is inwardly receiving the Word of God, it is 'feeding on Christ'. Jeremiah said, 'When Your Words came, I ate them' (Jeremiah 15:16). Meditation is receiving revelation of truth through the Word, by the Holy Spirit. The Lord Jesus said of the Holy Spirit: 'He will guide you into all truth' (John 16:13). We should be dependent on Him, not on our own understanding. The Holy Spirit is the best teacher and He will teach you as you rely on Him.

SIT WITH THE LORD

We find wonderful instruction in how to meditate in the well-known story in Luke 24, when the two on the way to Emmaus were joined by the resurrected Jesus, whom they did not recognize. When they came to their home, they invited the Lord in and He sat with them and they with Him.

Here is lesson one: Sit with the Lord. This means

an attitude rather than a posture. When we come to the Word or to prayer, we need to learn to 'sit' with the Lord. We need to hear from Him. Impressions come from four main sources – ourselves, others, God or the Devil. When we come to meditate, we want to hear His voice in the Word.

Quietly we trust the Lord to give us His thoughts as we open His Word. When we sit with the Lord, we can ask Him if there is anything in our hearts which displeases Him and, if so, to show it to us. If we confess our sins, He promises to forgive us. 'Jesus took the bread; gave thanks, broke it and began to give it to them' (Luke 24:30). This is what happens when we sit with Him, with our open Bible, to meditate. He takes the Word, blesses, breaks it and gives it to us and we receive it. We obey it. We respond to it and we inwardly receive it.

It is good to ask God to put His thoughts into your mind as to where to meditate. I strongly recommend you to ask God to put a particular book of the Bible into your mind. Start at chapter one, verse one, then go to verse two and so on. Meditate through the whole book, then ask Him for the next book.

One of the wonderful things about meditation is that the thoughts keep coming back. That is what is meant by meditating 'day and night'. This is the secret of an unsinkable life, having the constant scriptural presence of our blessed Lord and Saviour with us. You will discover by this means that 'glory and honour are in his presence' (1 Chronicles 16:27).

13

WHERE IS HE?

Solomon asked the question: 'But will God really dwell on the earth with men?' (2 Chronicles 6:18). And the Psalmist queried: 'Why should the Gentiles say "So where is their God?" But our God is in heaven' (Psalm 115:2–3).

In a student survey at one large British university, 81 per cent of the young people said they would like to know God personally. Job cried in frustration, 'Oh that I might find Him!'

The sceptic asked the missionary, 'You say you are saved, but how do you know?' With a glint in his eye, the missionary replied, 'Why bless my soul; I was there when it happened, so I ought to know!'

The prophet was challenged with the request, 'Is there no balm in Gilead? Is there no physician there?' In other words, is there no healer for our souls? No answer to our problems? No peace and ease for the confused and overwhelmed minds at the end of the twentieth century? The first question ever asked in the Bible was, 'WHERE ARE YOU?' (Genesis 3:9), and it is still being asked today. After Adam and Eve had sinned and hid themselves from the presence of the Lord, we read, 'the Lord God came walking in the Garden in the cool of the day and called to Adam, "Where are you?"' It was a question asked by God as He came in search of man.

The first question in the New Testament was that

asked by those wise men of the East when they arrived at Jerusalem: "Where is He?" (Matthew 2:2). This was a question asked by men when they came in search of God's Son. The answer was – in Bethlehem.

God's search for a lost mankind that had begun centuries before in the garden, had now brought him to earth. It was a journey that would take him to Calvary to die. But Christ did not stay on the Cross or in the tomb, He rose from the dead and then rose to heaven. So where is He now?

'In the midst of the seven lampstands, One like the Son of Man' (Revelation 1:13). Christ is no longer a babe in a manger or a man on a Cross, but a King on a throne. John sees the blinding splendour and awesome majesty of the triumphant Christ (Revelation 1:13–16). In his vision, the apostle not only describes His person, but also His position.

CHRIST AT THE CENTRE

What an encouragement that sight must have been to John and, later, to all believers, as they went through those times of opposition and persecution! They could rightly say: 'If this Jesus is with us, we can make it through whatever happens!' It was a sustaining presence. The sovereign Christ was at the centre of His suffering Church. It was a sovereign presence. What was true for the Church of the first century is also true for the Church of the twentieth century.

This great theme of Christ at the centre recurs throughout Revelation. The book places Christ in His proper place. He is the hub around which everything else rotates. Jesus is at the centre of the whole of history. In fact, as someone rightly said, 'History is

HIS STORY!' John Stott has said: 'No doctrine is truly Christian that does not have the Cross at its centre.' Michael Green, the Archbishop of Canterbury's secretary for evangelism, said: 'The Cross is at the heart of the Gospel.'

There was a little boy who always liked to be at the centre of attention. He heard two small boys arguing the other day. As boys do, they boasted about their possessions – bikes, computer games, toys.

The smaller of the two was obviously losing out. He thought deeply for a moment, then came up with something that totally silenced his companion.

'Anyway,' he yelled as he ran off, 'I've got tonsils – you haven't!'

But Jesus does not have to push His way in to make His boast. He stands by the wayside, on the side of the stage. His Name, His character, His glory, His love, His words are enough!

Christ is at the centre of God's great work of redemption. We are constantly reminded of this truth in the book of Revelation by the repeated description of Him as the 'Lamb'. He became the sacrifice for sin. He it is 'who loved us and washed us from our sins in His own blood.' (Revelation 1:5). In his Gospel, John records: 'They crucified Him and two thieves with Him, one on either side and Jesus in the midst' (John 19:18).

In Revelation, we see Jesus not only at the centre of His Church but also at the centre of the whole of history. He is called the Alpha and Omega, the beginning and the end. He had the first word in creation at the beginning of time, and He will have the last word at His coming at the end of time.

He is also at the heart of all that happens in between, for we are told: 'He upholds all things by the word of His power' (Hebrews 1:3). In the book of Revelation, He is 'in the midst of the throne' – the centre in time, space, earth, heaven and eternity. He is the beginning and the end, the Alpha and Omega, King of Kings, Lord Supreme. We are reminded in Scripture that He is: 'Christ, central in creation' (Colossians 1:15–18).

It's time to put him at the centre. It's the way to His immediate presence. It's the way to learning that it's the way through every storm, and to take the battle crown all the way through life. The way to finding that life is a piece of cake!

'Of course I'll get round to it … someday.' Yesterday, Lilian reminded me of my words when asked to paint the radiator. The radiator had remained unpainted.

Most of us have a 'someday'. Someday, we'll do something we'd always promised ourselves – visit Hong Kong, see the Taj Mahal, go on a cruise to the South Sea islands. Perhaps someday, we'll trace our family history, name all the galaxies, open an antique shop.

But sometimes the dream is better than the reality, I thought, as I dipped my brush into the paint pot …

Almost all our failure to settle our problems and master them is learning, knowing even, but not doing. We can dream, but it takes some effort to make those dreams come true.

OUR WORST ENEMY

It is more powerful than the combined armies of the world. It has destroyed more men and women than all the wars ever fought. It is more deadly than bullets and has wrecked more homes than the mightiest of bombs.

It spares no one, but finds victims among rich and poor alike. It lurks in unseen places and does its deadly work silently. You are warned against it, but you do not heed. It is relentless and it is everywhere, in the home, on the roads, in the factory and the school.

It brings sickness, degradation and death, yet few seek to avoid it. It destroys, crushes and cripples. It gives nothing and takes all. It is your worst enemy.

Its name is *carelessness*.

Some churches are full of the wrong emphasis. They are convinced they are right. After all, their churches are full, the people are coming in good numbers to their meetings, offerings are high, there are some conversions. It looks like success. The local fellowship has good music, fine programmes, social fads, feasting, conferences, seminars, counselling systems, even good prayers and occasional healings! But no marvellous presence. Where do you go to church and look around astonished in the UK today? Often there is no living Jesus, no mighty presence! Look at the bloodstained, dripping red Cross. Here is the amazing scene of the One who did not count it robbery to be equal with God, dying between two thieves. Christ on that central Cross was taking the penalty of our sin. God has only one plan to save mankind, and Christ is at the very centre of it.

In Revelation 1:10, John tells us he was 'in the Spirit on the Lord's day' when he had his amazing vision of Christ. Illustrated here is an important truth about the work of the Holy Spirit. The Spirit will always lead us to Christ. In John 16:14, Christ, speaking of the ministry of the Holy Spirit, says: 'He will glorify Me'. The acid test for every movement or individual that claims to be of the Spirit is – how much do they make of Him?

A true work of the Spirit will always be a Christ-centred work. John the Baptist was said to be filled with the Spirit from his mother's womb (Luke 1:15). It should come as no surprise then, that the motto of his ministry was: 'He (Jesus) must increase, but I must decrease.'

NOTHING SECOND-BEST

A mother and her young daughter were invited to a wedding. Towards the end of the reception, the little girl said: 'Is this all now, Mummy?' 'No,' replied her mother. 'We haven't had the toast yet.' 'Oh, Mummy!' exclaimed the little girl, 'I couldn't eat toast as well!'

God is not giving us second-best – but himself.

Marie Antoinette, Queen of France at the time of the French Revolution, when asked what the starving people must do, as they had no bread to eat, replied, 'Let them eat cake.'

The people are hungry and need the bread of life. Many today are being fed on fatty cake, the transient, the ear-tickling, that with no substance. The people need Christ Himself, His divine truth and Word. I remember that great Pentecostal preacher, the Reverend P. S. Brewster, saying to me: 'Melvin, nothing will stand but that done by the Word of God. All else will pass away. Only the Word of God will abide forever.' We want Christ Himself. He alone is sufficient for these trying times.

See the anointing on John the Baptist, who ushered in the Gospel age and was the forerunner of all evangelists, pointing to the first coming of Christ. The mark of John's success was not how many disciples he could gain himself, but how many he lost to Christ. He was not working to build his own little kingdom, but Christ's great kingdom.

So will every truly Spirit-filled man. When the Spirit fell upon the Church at Pentecost, the first thing the believers did was proclaim Christ to the crowds. A Spirit-filled Church will be a Christ-proclaiming Church.

SPIRITUAL CYCLONE

A Church that does not fudge, that is clear, plain, crisp and uncompromising will shake any community, anywhere, at any time. I was in a large Roman Catholic city in the South of Holland. No evangelists had seen the city moved before. The locals told me that the Roman Catholics just will not come into a meeting of another denomination. But a few began to come. Soon a spiritual cyclone shook the city. A Dutch newspaper carried a half page on the miracles and the people were very friendly. The place was filled to overflowing.

Tiny children with ash-white faces, who were very sick, were marvellously healed by our good Lord. A man, whom the best medical skills could not help, who could not carry his own weight since he was so ill, soon started running, and could carry a horse! The next day he walked miles and miles. Many were healed so that their lives were spared to see their families again. What happiness the Gospel is bringing!

Without miracles I am stranded; the people would not come. I was being filmed on video for French Television at the great Gospel campaign in the Congreshalle, Metz, a French city near the German border. The TV interviewer asked, 'How many of these people would come to hear you preach (there were 1,500 people nightly) if you did not have a gift of miracles to draw them?'

I replied, jokingly, 'Probably none of them.' But many came to Christ to be healed, and they heard and received His words. Jesus is the same today! We cannot succeed by word only, but in demonstration of the Holy Spirit and power. Paul agreed with that and said so.

The poster outside a Baptist church read: 'Try this church for a while. If you don't like what you hear, your sins will cheerfully be refunded!' But there is no refund for sin. You must mean business with God. We must have Him at the centre of our lives, for Christ central is Christ present.

Don't put it off. Don't say, 'Someday I'll reach this standard.' Some day is never. John Allan of Lyndhurst has enlarged the theme in a poem:

Some day, I'll be back home again,
Some day I will afford,
The fare – somehow I'll find somewhere,
Some day that train I'll board.

When life is easier, I'll return,
Some day when I've the time,
I promise that it won't be long,
When on that train I'll climb.

Some day I'll go, but not this week,
I'm busy every day,
But one of these fine days you'll see,
I'll tear myself away.

Some day I'll write a letter home,
I'll say I'm coming – soon,
Knowing well I've lots of time,
I'll make it May or June.

One day there came a letter brief,
The thing I'd dreaded most.
The bitter news, I was too late.
Sent to me in the post.

I would have gone some day I know,
How does one now explain?
I meant to come some time ago,
How does one ease the pain?

I'm on that train – my 'some day's' come,
I'm on my way to see,
Those whose 'some day' never came,
But will they welcome me?

THE SAVIOUR'S DAY

'Where is He?' was the question we began with. 'At the centre!' is the resounding answer that comes from the book of Revelation. There is, however, another more personal question we must ask ourselves. Where is He in my life?

It is possible to crowd Christ out of that central position He should have in our lives. This is true of the

Christians at Laodicea. In Christ's letter to that church in Revelation 3:20, He says: 'Behold I stand at the door and knock'. They had shut Christ out of their lives.

He is challenging you today! In Humphrey Bogart's famous phrase, 'This could be the beginning of a beautiful relationship'! Will you lock Him out? Or will you go on a magnificent journey through life with Christ? Cliff Richard's chart-topping Christmas singles, 'Mistletoe and Wine' and 'Saviour's Day', contain these challenging words: 'A time for forgiving, a time for believing, a time for striving and fighting to cease' ... 'for the Master is calling you on the Saviour's Day.' Christ says: 'I will not stand knocking forever, I'm moving on.' Don't miss Him. Keep Him in at your heart.

Jesus went on to say: 'If you hear my call and open the door, I'll come right in and sit down to supper with you, and the conquerors will sit alongside me.' What a wonderful promise of intimate friendship with Christ, to those who will give Him that central place in their heart!

'Whoever loses his life for My sake will save it' (Luke 9:24). Brahms, the famous German composer, had a weight problem, so his doctor put him on a diet. One day the doctor saw Brahms in a restaurant with all the wrong kinds of food spread out before him. 'So this is what you think of my advice,' he said to his patient. 'Oh,' Brahms responded, 'I've decided that it isn't worth starving myself to death just to live a few more years.' We may smile at Brahms' paradoxical reply, but there *is* a way to die in order to live.

A Christ-centred life cannot be self-centred life. Francis Ridley Havergall's words haunt me sometimes:

O Son of God, who lovest us,
We will be Thine alone,
And all we are and all we have
Shall henceforth be Thine own.

LIVE FOR HIM

A great Bible teacher said, 95 years ago to his generation: 'In only a few people is Christ prominent.' But
believers in Christ who deny themselves, take up
their Cross, and whole-heartedly follow Him do lose
their lives in the sense that they live for Him rather
than for themselves.

Thank God, a growing band are making the utter
sacrifice and are getting totally surrendered. Today a
mighty army of travelling believers and preachers
from every corner of the world is going from village
to village and house to house preaching the good
news of God's love. Why do they do it? For the
money? No, they receive almost no support for what
they do. Many are lucky if they have a bicycle, a Bible
and a change of clothes. Do they do it for fame and
fortune? There is none. In most cases only God
knows what good works these humble, sincere,
revived saints have done.

They do it because Jesus Christ is alive! He is living
in their hearts, and that Good News is something
worthy to share with the world. They are compelled
by the life that is in them to tell everyone that Jesus is
Lord. If Jesus Christ is not the Son of God, nothing
matters. But if He is, truly nothing else matters!

Is He knocking at your heart's door today? If
someone comes to your house and knocks on the
door, you can either open the door and invite him in,

or you can ignore the knock and he will go away. That's the way it is with Jesus knocking at your heart's door. You can bow your head on a bus, in a prison cell, in an office building, in a hotel room, in your hospital bed, or in the privacy of your home, and you can open your heart to Christ by a simple prayer of faith. Jesus Christ is the ultimate Good News. He is bigger than the Man of the Year. He is the biggest news story of all time!

Remember, he who abandons himself to God will never be abandoned by God! This is a secret of His continuous presence, and in that secret lies the reason why the true believer can say, 'It's all of Jesus! It's a piece of cake.'

14

GOD IS STRONGER THAN
YOUR STRONGEST FOE

Think more of the power of Christ in you than the power of sin over you. Man so often only has a small capacity to take from God. Thus many have a weak Jesus, a little God. As J. B. Phillips, Wiltshire's famous son and Bible translator, wrote: 'How small is your God?' Paul was able to say, 'The same was mighty in me!'

A lot of fishing stories are concerned with the big ones that got away. This little yarn takes a very different look at the subject. You can believe it if you like!

A man stopped his car to watch a fisherman on the river bank. First the angler hooked a large pike, and threw it back. Then he caught a beautiful trout, and threw that back, too. Then he landed a tiny perch, grunted with satisfaction, and put it in his bag.

The observer called out, 'Why on earth did you throw the two big ones back and keep the tiny one?'

Came the reply, 'I've a small frying-pan!'

Small visions, small minds. No victory. No success in life. No outstanding growth. Many are bored – they have no life, no real presence of our glorious, amazing Lord, no wonder or glory in their daily lives, no joy of the Christian walk. It's like the story of the small girl in church. It had been rather a long service in church, or so little Katie thought, and she was beginning to grow restless. Suddenly, in a quiet spell between hymns, her clear little voice piped up: 'Mummy, is it *still* Sunday?'

For me, Sunday, in fact every 24 hours of each day is not long enough to experience Him, to love and serve Him and feel the presence of the Lord Jesus Christ.

This is what the presence of Christ is about. A real Jesus. We have the same Jesus as yesterday, today and forever. 'The same Lord is rich to all who call upon Him' (Romans 10:12). Drunkards are made sober in seconds in this mighty glorious perennial presence. Adulterers are made pure. Broken homes are restored. Religious bigots are humbled and changed. What a difference to the Church, when Jesus – the same Jesus, not a different one – the same Lord is amongst us.

Have you a great measure of His presence? A great God? A tiny God?

GOD IS BIG

The Church will not survive as a credible force in the Western world without the miraculous presence of this BIG JESUS. Jesus promised, 'My Father and I will make Our abode with him.' God Himself is in us! The same grace, love, marvels, wonder, might and miracles are ours through this big God. God's own irreversible, incontestable declaration of intent is: 'Lo, I am with you always … '

He came down – a big God – to Moses in the Midian desert in a common bush. He came down to David in a cave. He came down to three faithful servants in the fiery furnace. He came down to Elijah in a still small voice in a lonely spot. He also came down to Paul and Silas as they sang songs in the night, and the bars fell away. And He came down to John on the island of Patmos, in his prison camp, with a revelation such as man had never seen before. We are still trying to fathom it out.

God is a big God. But no man is too small or insignificant for Him to visit, encourage, inspire, and help recover. He is big enough to be anywhere and small enough to be everywhere. Have a lot of room for Him in your life! Someone wrote to a friend:

> *Do not have a small capacity for God, but let:*
> *The Love of Christ surround you,*
> *The Light of Christ lead you,*
> *The Peace of Christ fill you,*
> *The Power of Christ assist you,*
> *The Joy of Christ thrill you,*
> *The Presence of Christ be with you always.*

A VISION NEEDED

'I saw the Lord ... then I said, "Here am I! Send me."' (Isaiah 6:1,8). In his book, *A Bunch Of Everlastings*, Frank W. Boreham writes about William Carey, the shoemaker who became a famous missionary to India:

> There he sits ... the Bible spread out before him, and a home-made map of the world on the wall! In the Bible he saw the King in His beauty; on the map he caught glimpses of the far horizon.

Our horizons are far too small! For many of us, the extent of our caring reaches only to our immediate family or to a small group of friends. What will it take to enlarge our perspective so that we become concerned about the lost in other lands? We need the same experience that motivated William Carey and the prophet Isaiah! Once they caught a glimpse of God's holiness, God's greatness, a vast God, an omnipotent and awesome King, a new vision came that opened up full capacity to Him. Cry today, 'Here am I!'

I recently came across these lines attributed to Francis Bacon, the poet and philosopher. They were written a long time ago, but are as true today as they were then:

> There is nothing purer than honesty; nothing sweeter than kindness; nothing warmer than love; nothing richer than wisdom; nothing brighter than virtue; nothing more steadfast than faith.

But what makes it work? You must receive the power of the Spirit daily to battle with the flesh in repentance, for this sort of triumphant living, to know strong victories over our foes. As Prime Minister John Major used to say of the fight against inflation: 'If it isn't hurting, it isn't working.'

James said, 'The trial of your faith is more precious than gold.' Smith Wigglesworth, one of the most successful and triumphant preachers of this century, said, 'Great faith comes from great tests ... and great victories out of great battles'. We must be fearless against unbelief, carnality – going to the Word of God again and again. One man who boasted he would move mountains fell over the first anthill he came across. We must be strong in the divine oracles of God.

'Greater is Christ in you than he that is in the world' (1 John 4:4). Often, when up against much opposition, I give that Scripture my own translation. I walk about quoting aloud to myself: *Greater is Christ in me now than in the foes that surround me.* It gives me a breakthrough every time.

He is greater than your every enemy. He is greater than your every force that opposes you. He is greater than your every test and power against you.

No! This does not mean life is rosy, but rather that this battle is His. I lean on Him. This philosophy from the Bible means that I've learned that I get quickly through hard places and patches which soon give way to the Holy Spirit when I stand four square with the omnipotent God. Repentance is the way to the mighty power and experience I'm talking about. With the Holy Ghost, it's a piece of cake. He wins for us. But it costs.

NO ROOM FOR WEEDS

An elderly man, who grew an amazing amount of food in a small garden, said, 'I have little trouble with weeds because I leave them no room. I fill the ground with healthy vegetables.'

I tried his formula a few years ago when I found the weeds out-growing my Impatiens. After pulling out the weeds, I added another box of flowers and watered them well. I had to uproot a few weeds, but the flowers soon took over, leaving no room for unsightly vegetation.

'Walk in the Spirit, and you shall not fulfil the lust

of the flesh' (Galatians 5:16). Fill your mind with holy, fresh, clean, happy, positive things. Fill it with Scripture. Keep pace with the mind and the thinking of the Holy Spirit. Beat the foe – by repenting!

Repentance is the first step to the anointing of the Holy Spirit. It must occur in every sinful action of your life, even in simple things – such as repenting if you haven't prayed, repenting if you haven't read the Word, repenting if you have neglected the Lord, repenting if you have lightly treated the awesome gift of the presence on your life, repenting if you have removed Jesus from your conversation.

Any of these sins show you are empty and dead, or at least on the way there. They disappoint the only One who counts. And there are much worse ones, which you know as well as I. They're more direct, often gross, sometimes vile. And naturally they must be dealt with, and quickly.

How do you do it? You go to God and you say, 'Lord, give me a repentant heart.' Like David, you say, 'Create in me a clean heart, O God.' You say, 'The sacrifices of God are a broken spirit, a broken and a contrite heart.' You say, 'Forgive me, Lord, for seeking the things of this world.' You say, 'Forgive me, Lord, for leaving my first love.' You say, 'Forgive me, Lord, for being so lukewarm.' You say, 'Take not Your Holy Spirit from me.' As Benny Hinn puts it:

Good friends, we must say to the Church – to ourselves – 'Get back, get back to repentance with a true heart.' We must start living the kind of life that is crucified with Christ daily, for if we do, we won't be able to keep the Holy Spirit away. We won't even have to ask Him to fill us.

Repentance fills our life with God's light. 'Arise and shine, for thy light is come, and the glory of the Lord is risen upon thee' (Isaiah 60:1). I wonder if you know the story of the father who willed that his fortune should be left to the one of his three sons who should most successfully fill a room with anything that cost no more than a shilling.

One son tried to fill it with old bricks, but managed to fill only a very small part. The second son bought straw, the cheapest thing he could think of, and managed to fill half the room. The third son bought a small candle, and filled the room with light.

The little verse I learned recently has these lines:

Though Satan may be given power,
  To carry out his goal,
We know that in our darkest hour
  Our Lord is in control.

As you move towards the presence of the Holy Spirit, I want to turn to a fact that stands behind everything we're talking about, especially the first step of repentance.

In the Bible, pointing towards the first coming of the Messiah, the prophet Zechariah says: 'As for you also, because of the blood of your covenant, I will set your prisoners free from the waterless pit' (Zechariah 9:11). God, talking about His people, is saying that the blood of Christ, the blood of the new covenant, will set them free. And the sad fact is that many people have no clue as to how they can and should apply the blood to their lives and receive the

146

liberty of repentance and all the truths of the faith.

Many are still bound. Demons harass them. Sickness has hit them and their children. Confusion is destroying their peace. Ephesians 1:7 says, 'In Him we have redemption through His blood.' We are redeemed by His blood, but redeemed from what? From the kingdom of darkness, the kingdom of Satan, who for now is allowed to rule the world. Christ knowingly *shed* His blood – he did not accidentally *spill* it – and redeemed us, bought us back. You can look Satan in the eye and tell him he has no control over you, for you were legally bought back.

The Blood speaks of the poured-out life. God recently gave me words from the throne, that the two emphases for His Church in the next few years, the last years of this century would be: 'The Greatness of God, and The Might of the Blood of Jesus.'

THE POURED-OUT LIFE

He bled to death. More battles have been fought, illogical, theological, ideological, nonsensical and idiotic, over this one truth than any other in the Bible. The humanists, atheists, and agnostics have banged their heads and worn themselves out opposing this great biblical fact. Today these people are no longer the danger. They are fading away. Muslims, however, continue to deny the crucifixion, death, blood and Resurrection of Christ.

The atonement is the perfect plan whereby a sinner might be made one with God. The old hymn that, as a lad, I used to blast out in Salvation Army Gospel meetings, went like this:

What can wash away my sin?
  Nothing but the Blood of Jesus.
What can make me whole again?
  Nothing but the Blood of Jesus.

It is the blood inside you that gives you life. If you go to the doctor for a good check up, he will take a sample of your blood. If it comes back clear then you are healthy. It is the blood of the atoning Christ that gives the Christian-faith 'life'.

Without the Blood of Christ we have nothing to offer the world. In thousands of crusades in 34 nations of the world and five continents, I have held up the bleeding form of Jesus Christ, as God's ultimatum for sin. The blood does a deep work. It cleanses the soul and mind. Every image is thrown down. No more nightmares about death and hell. The past is gone and God never recalls it as the blood has dealt with it – you have a new dimension. You are blood-marked. No power of hell can stand against the blood.

THE PLAN OF REDEMPTION

God's plan is the finished work of Calvary. It is wonderful to be redeemed or bought back. For 'you are not your own. You are bought with a price'. You cannot be redeemed by education. President Franklyn D. Roosevelt said: 'If we educate a man in his mind only we educate a menace to society.' Man needs changing.

I was preaching on the University of East Anglia campus for two healing services. This had never been allowed before in that establishment. It was crowded, with many new people. Many sick and disabled people came for prayer. But one night a group of students messed about at the back of the long hall, swinging from the door posts like monkeys, laughing, and making an awful noise. Some, no doubt, had had too much alcohol. I pointed them out and everyone turned to watch them. 'That's what you pay your taxes for,' I said. 'That's higher education. That shows you that intellect cannot give you manners, or make you civil, or save your soul.' I was greatly applauded by the large crowd.

Religion cannot save us. It was the most religious of people who demanded that Jesus be crucified – the Pharisees. It was religious people who stoned Stephen and imprisoned Peter. Religion can be very bigoted, snobbish, and very obnoxious and anti-christian. It can add burdens and not release them.

An old Indian Guru was visiting the so-called sacred river where it was stated your sins could be washed away. He came on his seventieth visit. He washed and came up out of the water, still the same. Then he saw a Christian believer, giving out Gospel tracts. The Christian's face shone. He was one who lived close to Christ in prayer. The old man, still with no inner peace, asked the radiant Christian: 'Tell me the river where you were washed and cleansed.'

He told him: 'In Christ's Precious Blood!'

As Paul wrote: 'But now in Christ Jesus you who sometimes were afar off are made nigh by the Blood of Christ' (Ephesians 1:7).

We used to sing as boys in the Sunday school:

> *There is power, power, wonder-working power*
> *In the blood of the Lamb*
> *... in the precious blood of the Lamb.*

The Blood of Jesus has the power to cleanse, deliver, free, change, release, purify, add peace and extend life.

I never fully understood the Scripture in Proverbs 20:30 about the bruise healing, until recently. I was re-reading it again: 'The blueness of a wound cleanseth away evil.' Bruise? Black and blue? A nasty wound? What on earth did it all mean? When I knock myself and a red patch or bruise appears on my body, my wife always humorously quotes her grandmother who always said, 'It's all the badness coming out.' But checking medically, and with Bible teachers, that is exactly what it means! The doctors say that the blue is the rich oxygen of the arterial blood that brings in new supplies and healing materials from the body's 'first aid kit'. Then red venal blood carries out the damaged cells, refuse and waste products. This is the red and blue sore patch on your leg, or arm, or any other part of the body. It's coming out – all the bad parts!

Jesus' Blood has the same two-fold healing purpose. It cleanses us of sin and waste, and it brings in the freshness of His love and Spirit into our lives. It does more than make us whiter than white – like the blueness of a wound, the bruise brings in new properties. We are regenerated, renewed in the mind, raised from spiritual deadness to Resurrection and new life. Making us thus pure, completely turning us into the temples of God. The curse of the Pharisees was that they were outwardly clean, impeccable, but inside they were like 'dead men's tombs', as Jesus said. The Blood of Jesus works inside us like a bruise, pushing badness, carnality, sin, and unrighteousness out, making us temples of life!

Let His Blood sink into your heart. Pray and ask Him, seek Him, say *sorry*, apologize to God. Moment by moment, your past is buried, gone forever. The Blood has swept it all away. You are new, brand new, perfect, clean and free.

I was baptizing some 21 eager young converts in a packed Gospel meeting in Germany recently. One skinhead, now saved and off drugs, clean, radiant with Christ, leapt and nearly jumped into the pool as he told of his wonderful fresh, clean, drugs-free life now.

'Much more having been now justified by His Blood ... we shall be saved from wrath' (Romans 5:9). Again, 'I am He who blots out your transgressions. I will not remember your sins any more ... state your case ... that you may be acquitted' (Isaiah 43:25–26).

HE CAME TO PLEAD FOR US

During the American War of Independence, George Washington was friendly with a minister called Peter Miller. Miller had an enemy in the town where he lived, a man called Michael Wittman, who did everything he could to oppose him.

Wittman was eventually arrested for treason and sentenced to death. When he heard what had happened, Miller walked 70 miles to Philadelphia to plead for his life. He begged Washington to give Wittman a pardon and set him free.

'No, Peter,' said Washington, 'I cannot grant you the life of your friend.'

'My friend!' exclaimed Peter. 'He's the worst enemy I have.'

Washington looked at him in amazement. 'You have walked all these miles to save an enemy? That puts a different light on the matter – I will pardon him!'

From that day, Wittman was no longer Miller's enemy but a true friend.

Jesus wants our deepest commitment and heart's devotion. C. H. Spurgeon told about the deep love and devotion French soldiers had for their leader Napoleon. He noted that it was not at all unusual for a mortally wounded soldier to raise himself up on one elbow and give a final cheer to his revered General. And if by chance the dying man saw Napoleon nearby, he would, with his final breath, shout, 'Vive l'Empereur!' Perhaps one of the most eloquent expressions of all, however, came from the lips of a soldier who had been shot in the chest. As the surgeon was attempting to remove the bullet, the suffering man was heard to whisper, 'If you go much deeper, Doctor, you'll come to the Emperor!' Spurgeon commented, 'He had Him on his heart.'

If a man as notorious as Napoleon could be the object of such undying devotion, how much more Jesus Christ, our Saviour and Lord! He was the sinless Son of God who willingly left heaven's glory to redeem lost sinners like you and me.

15

WHAT TO DO WHEN
NOTHING SEEMS TO WORK

Unbelievable, yet true; bizarre, yet it happened. A sixteen-year-old girl was kidnapped and held prisoner for four months. Where? In the attic of a church in Memphis, Tennessee.

Week after week that congregation gathered to worship, to sing, to pray, to enjoy Christian fellowship – and for four months in that very same building there was a terrified human being needing to be rescued. Until she was discovered and released by two men on the church's maintenance staff, that girl was a helpless captive.

Are you in that position today? A captive? You are a Christian of course, but you long to go higher for God, deeper in Him. You cannot move from where you are to where you long to be. You are a captive where you are! Many say, 'It just does not look like anything is going to work.' Matthew 17:14–20 tells of a needy man who approached Jesus' disciples for help. It records:

And when they were come to the multitude, there came a certain man, kneeling down, saying, 'Lord have mercy on my son, for he is a lunatic . . . I brought him to your disciples and they could not cure him' . . . and Jesus rebuked the devil and he departed out of him. And the child was cured from that very hour.

Here was a great need. The man brought the sick child to nine of the twelve disciples (three were on the Mount of the Transfiguration, praying). Here were the most God-blessed healing evangelists in the world at that time, yet none could do anything. Have you tried to pray and found silence? Have you been in the valley while everyone else is on the mountain top? Does nothing seem to work? Others prosper but not your family? You are still sick? But when Jesus comes on the scene every demon, every sickness, every trouble, soon leave. 'Rest in the Lord, and wait patiently for Him' (Psalm 37:7).

WHEN GOD PUTS YOU ON HOLD, DON'T HANG UP!

I'm sure you've had it happen to you. You call the appliance store and ask for the service department. 'Can you hold?' a cheerful voice asks, and before you know it you're hearing music. Every so often a taped message assures you that your call will be answered. You wait and wait. You think, *I could have driven over there and back by now!* You feel forgotten and that nobody cares.

Sometimes it seems that God has put us on hold. We pray and pray about a matter of extreme importance, but nothing happens. Nothing! I'm sure that's how Hannah felt. She was asking God for a baby. Childlessness was a curse in her day. To make it worse, her husband's other wife ridiculed her mercilessly. Hannah wanted desperately to give her husband a child. She prayed out of deep pain and bitterness. Year after year she did not conceive.

How can we reconcile the apparent silence of God

to our repeated prayers? Remember that God's wisdom surpasses our own. What we're asking for might harm us. We can't see the whole picture. Our timing is not God's timing.

When God puts you on hold, don't grumble. You can entrust your most cherished longings and desires to Him, and then patiently wait for Him to answer.

I remember that nobody wanted to work with the youth in that wasteland of Westgate Hill in Newcastle – a wild place. Recently there have been riots and street fires. There were no offers to evangelize, not one; it was so tough. So I had a go, and 200 hissing, baying, screaming, spitting kids were my congregation. But from teaching the Word of God to these coarse kids, I've been able to teach thousands in around 34 nations of the world! Have you given up the Sunday School? Have you shunned the little church, the small meetings? Have you run away from your anointing? 'You are not to leave the tabernacle of His Presence … and they did as He commanded' (Leviticus 10:7).

We must not walk away from the presence of Christ. Samuel was the great prophet, but King Saul, because he was impatient, could not wait. He made an offering himself, and stepped out of his calling. He did the priest's holy duty, and as a result he was demoted and lost his kingdom. We lose all by disobedience, by going our own way, by walking outside of our anointing and vocation.

David was anointed to fight wars. He was a warrior. But he was not called to build the mighty temple. Solomon was not called to fight battles but to build God's house, the Temple (2 Samuel 7). David wanted to build the temple however. And even the

God-blessed prophet Nathan thought it was a 'good idea'. But he misjudged. God said 'No'. It was not David's privilege. Keep in your anointing. Take time with God. Do what He tells you.

WHAT TO DO WHEN NOTHING SEEMS TO WORK

Many run away after waiting years for His place for them, and years later they are still getting nowhere. Nothing works. Their lives will not tick.

There are seven main principles to action when nothing seems to work. I shall deal with the first six of them briefly, and the last in a little more detail.

Look into your heart and life, and see if all is well with God.

Read through God's promises carefully. Make sure you know and understand them.

Confess with your lips. Let the Word of God become a way of life to you.

Are you in the wrong place? It is no good a bricklayer trying to be a clerk, or a painter being a car mechanic.

What are your companions and friends like? Who are you associating with?

Are you obeying God, and the Scriptures?

Are you living a life of praise and thanksgiving?

1 LOOK INTO YOUR HEART

Look into your heart and see if you are on a truly right standing with your heavenly Father. The Psalmist said he looked 'to see if there be any wicked way in me'. Keep the spiritual airwaves open to God. Not like the man in a remote African tribe who purchased a small radio for the first time when they came out. He had heard the music and voices on others' sets, but when he switched on he could hear only a crackling sound. He finally threw it away in disgust. But he had not touched the tuner or put the aerial up. A simple few seconds and he could have had power, songs, music, sound, life. He threw it away, although it had cost him six months' wages!

DON'T QUIT. Your faith can see you through. Keep open to God, and keep a clean heart. Stay switched on to Jesus. Keep in touch.

2 READ GOD'S PROMISES

Read carefully God's promises. They are many – 30,000 in Scripture. Listen to the Word. Read it. Study it. Write Bible verses out. Learn His promises. Scripture tells us: 'His promises are YES and AMEN to those who believe.'

God's Word will never change and never fail!

3 CONFESS WITH YOUR LIPS

Confess with your lips the words from the Bible, and your aims before the Lord each morning, each day. The woman who touched the hem of Jesus' garment said, 'I will but touch and be made whole.' She made up her mind. She said, 'I will reach this man, Christ. I will get to my goal.' When nothing works, say 'I will', and do it.

On television, millions watch the big matches

between the giants of the Premiere League, like Manchester United and Newcastle United. The titanic struggles between forty million pounds' worth of players for ninety minutes draw thousands of spectators. The players are given all sorts of advice. Everyone watching will give their views: 'He shouldn't have missed that one!' 'A bad move,' 'He should have hit it sooner!' 'That was bad. How could he have missed? I would have done this, that or the other.' Plenty of advice, but it's easy when you are not in the battle, when you're not on the pitch.

It's different on the pitch! It's not words but the execution of the Word. Put it into action. Get the critics on the field and they would match up very poorly. You must be fit. You must be up to it. You must be in it. Faith must have arms and legs. James said: 'I will show you my faith by my works.' Go practice the word. Use the corresponding actions to your words. In faith, it is actions that go with the sayings.

In Acts 3:19, Peter said to the people, after the mighty miracle of the man, lame since his mother's womb, was healed, 'Why look at us, as if we by our holiness and efforts did this … it is Christ.' Yes, it is the Lord of Glory. But as He sends His Word we must go and use it, and He uses us for His own honour.

4 ARE YOU IN THE WRONG PLACE?

Are you battling Satan in the area of reason? Stop! Get into the realm of faith. Fight! 'The battle is not yours, it is the Lord's!' Faith is the substance of things hoped for. Faith in the Lord Jesus Christ brings victory all the time. I've seen it for forty years.

Faith is the evidence of what you do not see with your eyes or feel with your senses.

Don't despise your gift or place or talent. If I walked out of my anointing today I would have nothing. God has this one place only for me, to win souls, to save the lost. It burns in me day and night, and night and day. Stay in your calling. God will increase what we have if we stay in the calling, in the blessing, in the anointing He has given.

Korah, in the Old Testament, wanted something else. He did not appreciate his sacred position in God's plan. He cried: 'I want to be like Moses.' He despised what he had received. 'Does it seem small to you that God chose you to stand before the people to minister to them?'(Numbers 16:9)

Stay walking with God. Stay in the perfect will of God. Don't go and mess it up. I cry to God early every morning: 'Give me your Word for today. Keep me clean. Don't let me fall into any snare. Don't let me despise my high calling. Don't let me mess it up. O God, keep me pleasing you.'

Take time to find out where you are and where God is taking you. People are in such a panting fever-ishness and rush that they miss God's planned job for them. Don't quit! Don't run away!

I like the poem I saw on a wall calendar in Kent. It goes like this:

Take time to think – it is the source of power.
Take time to read – it is the foundation of wisdom.
Take time to play – it is the secret of staying young.
Take time to be quiet – it is the opportunity to seek
    God.
Take time to laugh – it is the music of life.

Take time to dream – it is what the future is made of.
Take time to pray – it is the greatest power on earth.
Take time to love and be loved – it is God's greatest gift!

'Though a man live a thousand years twice over, but does not find contentment, well what is the use,' says Ecclesiastes 6:6. To please the Lord. This is our highest responsibility. Don't despise what you have.

You see it all over the place. Great cooks being waiters when they should be in the kitchen. Young men who love and were brought up to love farming and wide open spaces spending their days in a stuffy city office because they think that is the way to sophistication. Thousands of people in the wrong jobs! Do the job God has given you.

Whatever you are – be that,
Whatever you say – be true,
Straightforwardly act – be honest, in fact
Be nobody else but you.

Many people want to be somewhere else, but not where God wants them. God has said to me many times: 'Guard that gift. Be careful with that gift. It's not yours, it's mine. I've loaned it to you.' I've never desired to be elsewhere. I've always rejoiced in what God has given me.

I've stayed within the gift of healing, the gift of working of miracles, evangelizing the masses. Don't misuse what God has given you. David was accused by Nathan the prophet of the misuse of God's gift. 'Did I give you too little … wherefore have you despised the commandment of the Lord?' (2 Samuel 12:8) Do not despise the task, the job you have, your talent, gift, opportunity.

The grass looks greener in the other field. But it is just as tough! God will give you more if you appreciate what you have from him now. 'He that is faithful in least is faithful in much' (Luke 16:10). Start where you are. Guard that. Be satisfied with what God has given you. Don't complain. Work well and He will promote you.

Have you ever seen a round peg trying to get in a square hole? It happens every day. The speaker rises to speak with the words, 'Now I'm no speaker, but ...' Twenty minutes later (or even less), it is obvious to everybody that he is just exactly what he said he was – no speaker! Much better to be thought a fool than to open your mouth and remove all doubt.

We all know a gift when we see it. A gift does not need a trumpet to draw attention to its qualities. It is as clear as day. A gift always makes way for itself. You have a gift given you of God – use it! Don't, for any sake, try to be somebody else.

Seek to be in the right place. I've had many young men sent to me for training as evangelists. For some, the moment they arrive, they blunder and fail, making mistakes here, there and everywhere. But it is clear that they are a square peg in a round hole. It's not their calling. They can win souls, work in the Church, perhaps be a pastor or a song leader or drummer, but they are not called to a healing ministry or to be a New Testament evangelist. Yet another one has it as soon as he or she gets through my front door. He will do the tiniest job. He will clean the toilets, wash my car, write out envelopes.

161

Then he will usher at the door of the great meetings. Then he will counsel, lead the singing, read the Word to the densely-packed audience, then preach, lay hands on people, and miracles happen. Humbly, step by step, he develops. Soon he is out shaking the cities himself without me. Make sure you are in the right place with God.

5 ARE YOU OBEYING GOD?

Jesus said, 'Whosoever is a doer of the Word, I will liken him to a wise man who built his house on a rock …' (Matthew 7:24). 'Do not let the sun go down on your wrath.' Learn to forgive. Turn to the devil and resist him. He will run from you. Obey God!

6 LIVE IN PRAISE AND THANKSGIVING

Jesus praised *before* He raised Lazarus from the dead; Abraham praised God *before* he saw Isaac; Joshua and God's children shouted and praised triumphantly *before* the walls of Jericho came tumbling down. Praise God as if you have it, as if it is working then you *will* have it!

7 WHAT ARE YOUR COMPANIONS LIKE?

I believe that this is the most important thing to look at when nothing seems to be working. What are your friends, associates and companions like? I have found this to be by far the largest, single hinderance to finding things don't work. Anointing comes by association. To make it work we must be influenced by the godly, sweet, prayerful, Spirit-touched people.

What do we do when nothing seems to work? Find the right companions. Mix with the mightily anointed ones. Iron sharpens iron, anointing rubs off onto others. I remember when I sat in my first ever Pentecostal meeting in Newcastle upon Tyne and saw the Welsh evangelist, an old man of God who had come from the 'ark' to me. So old-fashioned, so blunt, yet so new and fresh to a young man's mind. He had been with the pioneers of the Pentecostal movement, Smith Wigglesworth, the Jeffrey brothers and others. He held me fascinated, laying hands on two deaf and dumb twins, and hearing them speak and talk and seeing them hear for the first time.

An anointing came on me from that mighty man of God. Who do you mix with? Don't criticize, don't find fault with the anointed ones. Billy Graham was blessed through the fiery Baptist evangelist Mordecai Ham. Benny Hinn was moved through Kathryn Kuhlman's life. Billy Bray was motivated through John Wesley's revival.

Gipsy Smith, the 'Billy Graham' of England during the time of the First World War, came from poor Gipsy campers. He was actually born in a wood under a tree. He could not even read or write till he was an adult. But his rise under God's anointing was meteoric, and he shook the nation, winning tens of thousands to Christ. He had been greatly influenced while a young Salvation Army Officer by the legendary William Booth, and the anointing rubbed off onto him. The fire and holy flame from Booth stirred young Gipsy Smith, and he never looked back.

Evan Roberts was won to Christ and first taught the deep things of God under godly, West Wales local evangelist, Seth Joshua, a man who possibly never left that principality. Yet the heavens fell on his prodigy, Evan, who saw the greatest revival of Christianity this century in the British Isles and touched the whole world.

In Scripture, Elisha received a mantle from Elijah. Solomon followed David in the anointing. Timothy had a legacy of power from his mother Eunice and his grandmother Louis. It can rub off. 1 Samuel 22:2 tells us of David's army – those who came to fight with him in God's cause. They were a motley crew; the outcasts, the failures, the scum of society. 'And everyone who was in great distress, everyone who was in debt, and everyone who was discontented gathered to him.'

Look a few years later – what a transformed, changed, anointed, powerful, God-touched band. This is what we read in 2 Samuel 23: 'These are the names of the mighty men whom David had ... Abishai the brother of Joab ... was chief. He lifted his spear against 300 men and killed them ... and had great honour ... ' 'Benaiah ... the son of a valiant man ... went down and killed a lion in a pit ... and won a name among the mighty men.' Also, 'He was called Adino the Eznite, because he had killed 800 men at one time.'

Look at the difference. Look at what they became through association with David, the mightily anointed man of God, the sweet, prayerful, godly man who was named as 'the man after God's own heart'. These fickle, feeble, weak, outcasts, who were at rock bottom, spent a short time with David, the choicest of God's servants. And soon they are enthused, healed of their hurts, remade, reborn, re-motivated, re-habilitated, re-built, ransomed, healed, restored and forgiven. They became mighty men of valour.

Association with those anointed, full of God's gifts and power – shaking towns, moving mountains by gladiators faith, crossing rivers that are uncrossable, bearing much precious fruit – can only stir you to your soul, rub off, cover you, overflow in you, and shape your life for eternity.

Reach out! Get in the way of God's outpouring of blessings. Don't let the anointing pass you by. Seek fellowship with those saturated in the presence of God.

BY FAITHFULNESS

Our anointing increases as His presence increases, as He sees our longstanding faithfulness. The man with the ten talents, the five talents and the one talent in the Bible story received accordingly as they responded to what was in their hand. The one who buried his one talent and did nothing received only God's condemnation. The man despised his one talent and did nothing with it, so lost all he had. 'He that saveth his life shall lose it.'

Use what you have. Spread the Good News. Be faithful to His commands. Give to the poor. Don't contain. Don't be selfish. Don't keep the Good News to yourselves. Give your talent away. Use what you have for others. Give yourself away to be used by God. Be faithful to His instructions. 'He that loseth his life shall save it.' There is a price to pay. Say it today and every day: 'The increase of His presence depends on me ... '

What will you do with your call, your talent, your opportunity? He has promised us victory in the battle He has already won.

Do not miss His presence. Catch the vision. Seek His face. Grasp hold of the dream. Love His presence. Be faithful to His Word, and 'He will direct you in all your ways'. Failure to possess the land cost Art an untold fortune. Don't miss His presence.

He loves faithfulness. It takes discipline to go and listen and learn from others. Many preachers miss a revival by not humbling themselves to do so. If I hear God is using a younger preacher, or indeed anyone, I may never have heard their name, but I will jump in my car and drive many miles to get a blessing, to be re-quickened, be refreshed, to get something of their anointing by association.

We must be faithful to seek contact. We must be modest and humble ourselves. Many dry up as they lose faithfulness in persisting in firing up their anointing by touching others and receiving from others.

Brother Reinhard Bonnke, who has reached millions with the Gospel of Christ, discovered a great blessing from the faithfulness of his father, a Pentecostal minister in Germany. Although he did not realize it, even his father's strictness and inhibitions drove him to seek the Lord, and eventually launched him on this mighty ministry.

God uses small, almost insignificant things to launch us into His will, into the harvest field, into His blessings. Reinhard Bonnke tells how, as a shy young man, he was much under his father's authority. His father was a strict but good pastor, who disliked anything out of order. One day, while in their weekly

Pentecostal prayer meeting, on his knees, God said clearly (Reinhard could not mistake it was God): 'Go and pray for that sick old lady in the corner before she leaves the church.' This would have been right out of order to do so in his strict Pentecostal Church. He loved his father and dared not disobey him and tackle that sort of demand. But God constrained him and pressurized him. He got up from his knees finally, as the meeting ended, and with great nervousness, thinking, 'My dad will kill me for this,' he went up and, shaking physically, laid hands on the lady and prayed in the name of Jesus for her healing. He was throbbing with divine currents of Holy Spirit power. His dad saw what was going on and was shocked. Walking up to him, he said, 'What are you doing to that sister, Reinhard?'

Before he could reply, the old lady spoke up, 'He prayed for me, Pastor, and I felt God's power, and I'm healed. All my constant pain has gone!!!'

His dad could say nothing and God's servant was launched! Obey God, His voice, His call, His whisper in your heart, even if you are shy, backward, slow, hesitant. God will work it out, not for your glory, but for His purposes!

We grow, we are anointed, we see things move again when nothing much has worked, when we gather closer to our blessed Saviour, when we keep good company with anointed servants of God, His presence, His will, getting things done at last in life by learning obedience and discipline from powerful, godly servants of the Lord.

16

THE PRESENCE OF CHRIST ON THE STREETS OF BRITAIN

In a tiny East Coast community not long ago, I was preaching for three days, and crowds came in such numbers that the local church was overwhelmed. 'What did you come to see – a reed shaken with the wind?' Certainly that word came true. The place, even with two meetings daily, became packed out. Long queues formed to get in – 90 per cent were unsaved people. God did wonders. One afternoon, there were many people thronging into the church building, and it was a cold March day. The wintry East wind was bitingly cold. Many sick people stood or sat in disabled chairs outside, unable to gain admission. My wife, helping to usher and accommodate folk, was also shut outside. There was not an inch left to spare.

She managed to get a hand-written note sent to me, to explain it would not be possible for these very infirm people to sit under such adverse conditions out there, or we'd be raising up dead corpses by the end of the day! Could I please get out and pray for them *on the street outside*. This I agreed to do. I had to be bodily lifted above the people's heads to get to them. Finally, when I got on the pavement, the press and photographers had arrived. They were about to have a field day with the evangelist. I could imagine the headlines: 'EVANGELIST KEEPS OLD AND INFIRM IN FREEZING TEMPERATURES'. But before they could get pen to paper, as I was laying hands on each sick person, I felt the presence of Christ. The mischievous works of the Devil were counteracted, and one after another cried out with relief as their pains dropped away.

One got out of a wheelchair, one danced, throwing off crutches. Sticks were laid down in the roadside. People hearing my loud prayers on the quiet street of the town came to their windows. Soon folk stood alongside the kerbside. This had never been seen on the streets of rural UK in living memory, I doubt. A wheelchair abandoned, another pushed off up the street. Chaos, noise, excitement. It was murmured about that *Jesus was in the street*.

Pain went. People shouted for joy. Mighty evidences of His personal presence were strewn along the footpath. People thronged. The press, no doubt forgetting the former headlines in their minds, were now positive friends and with us 100 per cent. As so often, won over by a whisker, they talked to folk, ran from one to another who had been cured, and were perspiring with near exhaustion trying to keep up with the miracles.

God was everywhere on that Lincolnshire street. It was miraculous, He was present. The cycle had come. God was visiting us. It's all a mystery, but I was learning how to be hungry, how to get into His presence, how to obey, how to please Him, how to keep in His presence. Once we are convinced the cycle is here, He is ever ready to constrain us, and fellowship with us, and to go with us. Anything is possible.

Secular Britain is reeling in parts with God's power. Someone once said of the average Englishman, 'More people in our society pray to God than who believe He exists.' Most people who are in their forties or fifties, who get through some serious problem or illness use the phrase later: 'It's my faith that got me through.' Lord Althorpe (Princess Diana's brother) said recently, 'I pray still.' Barry Norman, top film critic of the BBC and writer, confessed, 'Until my twenties I prayed ... I don't now. Maybe I should again.'

People are feeling their needs in these crushing days. Christianity is a religion of miracles. The Psalmist said: 'He sent His Word and healed them and delivered them from all their destructions' (Psalm 107:20).

When in the North of Scotland recently, the power of God swept my meetings in this very cautious part of the land. One local church leader told me, 'It's very many years since so many were converted in services here.' So many were healed that when the local countrywide newspaper men came to photograph and talk to folk, they queued up to tell them of their new health, miracle or healing.

One reporter asked me, 'What is your ambition now?' He commented that I had just about seen every miracle cure in the book (including the dead raised). What else could I hope for? I replied, 'To put the Devil out of business!' I have perhaps an even greater longing – to be like Jesus. But that lies in how much I have of the presence of Christ.

In Peterhead, the mighty blessings, healings and

salvations came because He – the Lord – was present. It is said that Kathryn Khulman carried the presence of Christ at His greatest in her life in the final ten years of her ministry. It was so great that when she went into a hotel people were healed as she passed by. As she went into a store to purchase something people were healed. Paul claimed, 'They that are Christ's have crucified the flesh with its affections and lusts' (Galatians 5:24). That is the secret to shaking towns by God's power.

HUMILITY

One broad, blunt Scottish lady said to me in one crowded meeting on the North coast, 'I like your meetings but I don't like you. You are too big-headed.' There had been some wonderful miracles in that afternoon's healing service. I thought I had done well. But this lady had not seen Jesus enough.

The next day in another powerful meeting she was present. She grabbed me as I was leaving: 'You were all right today, you were humble.'

I took the message right on the chin! Moses 'wist not that his face shone'. He had the glory of God, the presence of God, and he was deeply contrite. Adam tried to become like God and lost his communion, his relationship with God, and saw himself naked. He became very self-conscious. Soon he was hiding away from God. When King Saul was, 'small in his own eyes' he was great. When he 'hid himself away from sight', shy and embarrassed, he was chosen by God. When he (the Psalmist tells us) 'forgot God's works, he waited not for His counsel', he became hasty, disobedient, arrogant, and lost the presence of God

(Psalm 106:13). He ended up defeated and destroyed.

Cry out, 'Take not Your Holy Spirit from me.' I say it so often before a large Gospel Healing Crusade Meeting. 'Do not desert me, do not leave me, O Lord.'

STUCK TO THEIR SEATS

Mrs Woodrow had such an anointing and presence of the Holy Spirit, that people were stuck to their seats and could not move from the meeting. In Scotland I saw the whole congregation – including many sinners – struck to the ground and lay there prostrate, flat on their faces for hours, until one o'clock in the morning.

People have heard and seen angels in my meetings. A little child saw a great 'white man', beautiful and majestic, guarding me, standing behind me in a mighty, anointed meeting in Cornwall a few years' ago. In 2 Chronicles 7:2, the glorious presence was so great that people could not get into the temple. It records: 'The priests could not enter in because the glory of God filled the temple.'

In Wesley's and Finney's meetings there are records of people hitting, as it were, an 'invisible wall' of power and presence. Some fell under it, or groaned under it, and others could not enter into the services because of it.

I see people healed on the way to my meetings – some as they leave. Others are healed as they sit waiting hours before a meeting. Others are cured as they queue up to get into the gathering – healed on the streets outside!

God is teaching me. I am not often humble, I fail him a lot. He is patient with me. Self-centredness is the ruling spirit of this age. 87.8 per cent of book titles in Christian book shops last year, I noted, dealt with the 'I' and the 'Me'; with 'my image', 'my problems'. The self-centred life is popular. Here are a few titles: *Relax and Live Longer*, *How to Discover Happiness*, and *How to Become Your Best Self*!

Nowadays, it's what 'I look like', or 'feel like', that is all important. People say, 'I feel at peace about it,' or, 'I feel good,' or, 'I feel nice'. Maybe God is calling us to be uncomfortable, and speaking to us about a way that is costly. To move away from self to humility is vital.

Matthew 18:4 says, 'Whoever humbles himself like this child, is the greatest in the kingdom.' Psalm 149:4, 'The Lord takes pleasure in His people. He adorns the humble with victory.' Paul wrote, 'Honour one another above yourselves' (Romans 12:10). Martin Luther said, 'There came a day when I laid down my rights.' Remember his reply when asked what were the three greatest virtues of the Christian faith. He replied, 'HUMILITY, HUMILITY, HUMILITY.'

To the selfish and proud there is no victory, only touchiness, greediness, and a wounded spirit. Why? Because they worship at the shrine of the pampered and the self-pitied. It needs an inner crucifixion from self-infatuation, to be deeply united in God's love. For, 'If anyone thinks he is something, when he is nothing, he deceives himself' (Galatians 6:3). Martin Reynolds, of New Hope Bible College, Peterhead, put it in verse, entitled 'True Humility':

*True humility never says, 'I'm all right, I've got
    enough of it in me'*
*but goes on meekly to God each day in prayer
    to ask for more.*
*True humility never blames our weaknesses
    entirely on the faults of others,*
but admits our share of the blame.
*True humility never seeks to be nice or kind so
    as people will praise us for these qualities,*
*but instead uses them to attract people to Jesus,
    the life-giver and perfector of us all.*
*True humility is not just being emotional about
    Jesus,*
*but also seeks to grow daily into His likeness
    and meekness.*
*True humility never regards a job which
    requires more thought and intelligence as
    more important than a job which requires
    less,*
*but instead willingly and joyfully accepts any
    work that is given.*
*True humility never says 'No' to anybody who
    asks for any kind of help or hospitality,*
*but willingly forgets self and feelings to see
    another's needs met.*

GOD'S WORD – THE KEY

God's Word is victorious both in the humble and the
meek, and through them to the world. This is beginning to stir and shape whole communities in Britain
today.

On the wall of a lounge of an old people's home are
these words:

We were born before television, before penicillin, before polio shots, frozen foods, Xerox, plastic, and contact lenses. We were before credit cards, laser beams, ball-point pens; before dishwashers, electric blankets, tumble dryers – and before man walked on the moon.

We were before day-care centres, group therapy, and nursing homes. We had never heard of FM radio, tape decks, electric type-writers, artificial hearts, word processors, yoghurt – and men wearing earrings. For us, a 'chip' meant something that went with fish, hardware meant hardware, and software wasn't even a word!

No wonder we are sometimes confused, and that there is often a generation gap. The main thing is we have survived. Let's celebrate that fact every day!

God's Word survives and thrives. God never fails, never changes. He is the timeless truth of the ages. I liked the little story told by Lloyd Douglas, author of *The Robe*. One morning he met a violin-maker.

'Good morning,' the violin-maker said.

'What's good about it?' asked the author.

'Oh, this,' said the violin-maker as he picked up his tuning fork and sounded 'A'.

He struck it and said, "A' is 'A' today and it was so yesterday. 'A' will be 'A' a thousand years from now.'

So if you should fear anything in this quickly-changing world, remember the violin-maker's 'A'. Remember too that great truth, that God will always be constant – yesterday, today, and tomorrow.

I also like the story of the retired newspaper

columnist whose neighbours' young son was always catching him out with riddles and jokes. But this day he thought he had licked him. He wrote about the incident.

The lad opened up on me: 'Say, why did the orange stop halfway down the hill?'

This time I was ready for him. 'It had run out of juice!' I replied laughing, for it's not often I get the better of him.

He wasn't finished, though, for he asked another one: 'Ah, but how did the orange know the time it ran out of juice?'

I had to admit I didn't know the answer.

'It listened to the pips!'

It's time to listen to God. As John wrote, 'The world passes away, and the lusts thereof' (1 John 2:17), but His Words last when all else has gone.

GREAT EXPECTATION

The weekly worship and tradition is predictable in most churches – even in many Pentecostal and house church groups. The same things happen week after week after week. The Holy Spirit often departs and no one misses Him. Very rarely do you find a church that astonishes you any more. But God promised, 'Your expectation shall not be cut off.'

God is about to meet you with a high level of anointing and faith. God is about to visit His people with bread. Live in the Word. Live in expectation and hope. The Book of Psalms tells us, 'Those who are planted in the house of the Lord shall flourish in His courts'. Expect, obey, take the initiative. Grab the opportunity. Let God be with you to create the circumstances to take the moral and spiritual high ground of faith.

Keep away from the clowns who have lost that vital anointing and look good but are missing the Word of the living God for this hour. Remember the prayer of Martin Luther, 'O Lord, deliver me from my enemies and also, O God, deliver me from my friends.' Keep in with anointed, prayerful, loving friends.

Stay in prayer night and day, day and night. Be day and night in that attitude. We may not be on our knees every moment but keep in that spirit. God is a big God, we must ask big things of Him. Samuel of the Old Testament said: 'I will not sin in not praying for you.' The serene effort of prayer is the only power on earth that will lift man from his weakness, idolatry, failure, inertia into steadfast glory and blessing. If I fail in anything then it is because I have not prayed enough. If I am a notable success, then it is because in that matter I interceded and the Lord gave the increase. His is the glory. We have no power of ourselves. It is all His.

There was a little boy who was always talking about Jesus. One day, he said to his Mum, pointing at the shoe repair shop, 'Jesus is in there, Mum.'

His mother constrained him, assuring him Jesus could not be in the cobbler's shop.

'Oh yes, Mummy. Look at that sign in the window.'

It read: 'HEELING WHILE YOU WAIT'!

What an expectation! It is when we expect much of God's great power that we see the shaking and the trembling commencing.

17

FINISH WITH HIS PRESENCE

> Be steadfast ... in the work of the Lord,
> knowing that your labour is not in vain.
> (1 Corinthians 15:58)

A preacher who was growing weary in the ministry had a dream. He saw himself pounding away at a huge chunk of granite with a pick-axe. It was his job to break it into small pieces. But hard as he tried, he couldn't chip off even a tiny piece. At last, tired and disappointed, he decided to give up.

Just then a stranger appeared and said, 'Weren't you given orders to do that work? Your duty is to give it your best regardless of what happens.' The minister, with a renewed determination, grabbed the pick-axe, lifted it high in the air, and gave the granite a crushing blow. It broke into a thousand pieces. He had almost quit, just one blow too soon.

The Lord wants us to keep working at our God-given task no matter how difficult it might be. Even when success seems remote or impossible, we are to remain steadfast, assured that there will be an ample reward for those who persevere. Have you grown tired in your service for the Lord? Have you become so discouraged that you're tempted to 'throw in the towel'?

Never be a quitter. Failure is not defeat unless you stop trying. The poet put it like this:

We run with patience day by day
  By drawing strength from Christ our Lord;
And if we falter on the way,
  He will renew us by His Word.

IT'S ALWAYS TOO SOON TO QUIT

The name Mickey Thompson used to be one of the most recognized names in auto racing. His team built the fastest cars on the track. They could fly! But not one of those cars ever brought Thompson a chequered flag. That's right – although his cars took the lead in the first 29 races they entered, they never won a race. Why? Because they did not finish.

Thompson could make the fastest cars, but he couldn't build them to last. They all broke down during the race. Engines blew. Gearboxes broke. Carburettors failed. His cars were good starters and fast runners, but they were not good finishers.

As we run the race of the Christian life, we need to end well. The Apostle Paul is an example of a good finisher. He received Christ on the Damascus Road. He attended 'seminary' in the Arabian desert (Galatians 1:17–18). He served Christ in spite of hardship and persecution. He opened Europe to the Gospel, and at the close of his life, he could say with confidence: 'I've run hard to the finish, and believed all the way' (2 Timothy 4:7).

What about you? Has something stalled you in your Christian growth? Have you had a 'break-down'? Confess your sins, make the necessary repairs, and get back into the race. If you don't give up, Jesus will help you to be a good finisher!

A talented young protégé of a great piano teacher

was preparing for his biggest ever recital. Everyone in the music world who was important was to be there. At this top theatre, this was to be his great hour and moments of opportunity. He was very nervous standing in the wings waiting for his entrance. His noble teacher stood proudly by his side. In a moment, however, he would be alone with the world of stars. She, suspecting his nervousness and anxiety, whispered, 'If you make a mistake, don't worry. Just keep going. Remember, whatever happens, FINISH WELL!' He did just that, a brilliant performance, from which he never looked back. It launched him on a glittering career in the music world. But he never forgot 'FINISH WELL!'

GET UP AND GO

'I can make it through anything, in the One who makes me who I am,' wrote Paul (Philippians 4:13). We aren't born naturally skilful. We may be born with a talent, but whether or not it develops is entirely up to us.

'How did you learn to skate?' I once asked a competitor after she'd won a competition.

'By getting up every time I fell down,' was the reply.

And if we do just that, there's no telling what we can achieve at the end of the day. As Martin Luther wrote:

> *Did we in our own strength confide,*
> *Our striving would be losing,*
> *Were not the right Man on our side,*
> *The Man of God's own choosing.*

With Christ present we are urged on to the goal line, like a lady we heard of, called Dora. Dora has proved – with astonishing persistence and courage – the wisdom of the saying, 'If at first you don't succeed, try, try again.' She was in her late fifties when her husband died. She had never learned to drive, but decided she must do so at once. She took lessons, and eventually passed the driving test – but not before failing 18 times!

Each time she tried it she would get into such a state of agitation that she made foolish mistakes. What torture she endured! Many people would have given up trying, but persistent, courageous Dora overcame her nervousness at last and finally got through.

TAKE ANOTHER LOOK

Have you noticed that any lasting success has, more often than not, been achieved against a background of failures, setbacks and disappointments? It is how we meet these obstacles that determines our destiny.

A king once had a beautiful diamond. It was large and rare, and he was very proud of it. One day, the diamond was scratched and became so disfigured that none of the court jewellers would risk trying to remove the mark. The king became very unhappy.

Not long afterwards, a new young jeweller came to court. He examined the diamond carefully and promised that he could make it even better than before. The king was very sceptical, but he decided to give the man a chance, so he handed over the diamond. When it was returned to him, the king was amazed, for the craftsman had engraved a beautiful rosebud around the flaw, and the ugly scratch had become the stem. It was, indeed, more beautiful than it had been.

Sometimes we are all apt to think that something – a plan or a relationship – has been ruined. Instead of giving it up as a bad job, it's always worth taking another look. So often there is a way, not only of saving the situation, but of making it even better than before.

FINISH WELL

I know of a great Bible teacher in Ireland, who for 25 years held over a thousand people captivated every Tuesday night at his weekly Bible class. Saved from the gutter and drunkenness, he became an avowed believer. He studied the Bible, and answered the call to the ministry. He saw the most successful mid-week Bible study up until that time in the British Isles. He was vehement, particularly in teaching, however, against the Full Gospel Pentecostal churches. He hated the charismatic renewal, and in his Ulster bluntness tiraded against it. However, that aside, he did teach some solid truths from the Bible and was the apple of the evangelicals' eye in Ireland.

However, his ending was one of shame and scandal. He was found in his locked study with his brains blown out. He died by his own hand. It soon circulated that he had been womanizing with as many as two and three different ladies for some time. Friends claimed the IRA killed him but the door could hardly have been locked from the inside. A great ministry by and large, but all lost through an ignominious and scandalous ending. Finish well!

I know of possibly one of the greatest healing

evangelists of all time. As a young teenage preacher I followed his career. He had the biggest tent in the world, filling it with untold thousands. I witnessed 7,000 people go forward at one Gospel appeal for salvation. Radio and television carried stories and live pictures of paralysed people carried in on beds, at death's door, raised up in minutes as he prayed compassionately over them. He was anointed, powerful, genuine. However, his ending was that of a drunk. *The Times* newspaper reported him found dead in a motel of alcohol poisoning. He had been a secret drinker for some years prior to his demise. A great, noble, mighty soul-winner, but his finish did not glorify the Saviour.

I loved my mother, in my eyes she was perfect. Her prayers raised me from the dead when I drowned in the river at Weston, Somerset, in 1940. She brought me up faithfully in the Church, and saw the ministry become anointed and grow world-wide. She saw the miracles of healing and thousands come to our Lord Jesus Christ in my missions across this nation. She saw my books sell and bless thousands of people. She worked in the office with us for three decades. She never preached a sermon, but she could pray. I loved her deeply, and went to see her daily when home from my international crusades. She went to heaven in her 79th year suddenly and painlessly, only hours before I could get home from preaching overseas. She died with a smile. The words on her grave are:

When she was born she cried,
*   and the world rejoiced.*
When she died, we cried,
*   but Mum rejoiced.*

The newspapers carried the headline: 'GOD'S GREAT LADY DIES'. She finished gloriously!

PERSIST

One day a man, enjoying a hot afternoon on the beach by the sea, was troubled by a persistent bee. It kept coming at him, coming at him, fastening itself on him, and he got mad. He knocked it to the ground, and stamped on it. He then sat back in his deck chair, when some minutes later he heard that bee, buzzing and buzzing. It was coming at him again! He got really mad this time, hit at it, knocked it, and finally got it on the sand and stamped and stamped, till it had gone deep into the sand.

About half an hour later he heard a buzzing. He looked down. There was that bee. One wing had been put out of action, but it was struggling across the sand, licking itself, working on itself. This time he did it no harm. He just watched out of sheer admiration for it. And soon it propped the bad wing up, and was flying. It was out of direction due to its wounds, but it landed on a sand dune, and worked at itself. In 30 minutes it was flying weakly but almost at full go, buzzing and humming. But this time it left the man alone and went off in the opposite direction. But it persisted, it won – it found recovery. It never gave up. It finished well!

Try again. Have another go. Don't give up – there is always a way – start again. Pray through with God's will. With His presence we can go on to victory and finish fantastic! Stretch yourself, spread your wings, fly, take off for Jesus!

With Christ we have the victory. 'We are more than

conquerors.' He is able to save by many or few.

> *If God be for us, who can be against us?*
> *Let God be true and every man a liar!*
> *God is able to do exceedingly above all that you ask or think.*
> *The battle is not yours but the Lord's.*
> *Because He lives we shall live also.*
> *All things are possible to them that believe.*

The promise to the triumphant believer is from the divine oracles of God: 'They will receive ... the gift of righteousness and shall reign in life by one Jesus Christ' (Romans 5:17). It's all because of Jesus. He is all, He is everything. 'Now to Him who is able to do exceedingly abundantly ... be glory' (Ephesians 3:20–21).

It's the power that works. Lay hold of it and discover, as I have, that you *can* move the mountains in your life!

Due to the overwhelming response of thousands to the present awakening in the United Kingdom, through the commitment to God's guidance of the Rev. Melvin Banks, his family and their team, he personally or one of his family would be happy to make themselves available to visit your town, city, suburb, church or fellowship, in order to share these amazing stories and testimonies. Please contact the address given below.

The Rev. Melvin Banks welcomes letters, invitations, and prayer requests for you or your loved ones.

Also available are videos, audio tapes and free literature. For the latest news of the Revival send a stamped addressed envelope to:

The Rev. Melvin Banks
International Crusade Office
44 Monks Way
Chippenham
Wiltshire SN15 3TT
England
Telephone: (01249) 655712

If you would like further copies of this book, or other books by Melvin Banks – *Faith Unlimited*, *Expect a Miracle*, *Healing Secret*, *The Greatest Miracle*, *The Wind of Fire*, *With God All Things are Possible* – please ask at your local Christian bookshop.